BRINGING THE LIGHT INTO THE DARKNESS OF WORLD RELIGIONS

God's Great Commission

BRINGING THE LIGHT INTO THE DARKNESS OF WORLD RELIGIONS

God's Great Commission

by
Dr. William H. Hooppell

BRINGING THE LIGHT INTO THE DARKNESS OF WORLD RELIGIONS

God's Great Commission

The Scriptures used throughout this book are quoted from the *Authorized King James Version* unless otherwise noted.

ISBN 0-9743339-8-0
Library of Congress Control Number: 2005932712

Published 2005
Printed in the United States of America

Published by

HERITAGE INK

Marianna, Florida 32446
www.heritageink.com

Dedication

This book is dedicated to my precious wife, Annie, with all my enduring love. "For this reason a man will leave his father and mother and be united to his wife, and they will become one flesh" (Genesis 2:24).

Acknowledgements

Dr. Hooppell wishes to acknowledge his deepest appreciation to all those people who helped him in publishing this work.

To contact Dr. William H. Hooppell for speaking engagements, contact:

**Great Commission Ministries
7111 Birchwood Road
Grand Ridge, Florida 32442**

E-mail: whho@digitalexp.com

(850)592-8381

Contents

Contents (Continued)

Contents (Continued)

INTRODUCTION

Man is a curiously religious being. He continually searches for objects to worship that he may call "god."

It is the spirit of man that craves for an object to reverence, worship and adore, but it is his intellect that devises that object of worship. Consequently, man is being continually misled in his search for the true God to worship.

Like all mankind, I searched for a "god" to worship that would appeal to my various senses. I found none that would fit into the pattern of my life-style. One day however, I found the Lord Jesus Christ as my personal Lord and Savior. He did not fit into my pattern of life-style, but rather, I was transformed by the power of the Holy Spirit into conformity with the life of the Lord Jesus Christ. The search was over, for the spirit was satisfied.

There are a number of world religions today who have multi-millions of followers all searching for the truth. None of these religions offer the peace and security that is found only in Jesus Christ. The reader of this work may be a Christian witness who comes upon an adherent of one of these religions. Therefore, the purpose of this work is to help the Christian witness to be able to lead adherents to these other religions to a saving knowledge of the Lord Jesus Christ.

Since every life is of great value to God, then no life should be exempt from hearing the message of salvation. The Christian witness is not to be excused from witnessing to anyone on the grounds that he is ignorant of one's religious beliefs, philosophies, customs or culture. If he is lacking in such knowledge, then he should seek such knowledge from available sources of information that will assist him.

I have endeavored to present such a work that will help Christians understand the origin of the major world religions, their founders and beliefs, and to suggest possible methods that can be used in witnessing to the adherents to these world religions.

This work also deals with the beliefs of these world religions, and examines their similarities and dissimilarities with the Word of God. This will be of inestimable value to the Christian witness, for in the similarities of beliefs between the Christian beliefs as recorded in God's Word, and the beliefs in one of the world religions, he will have an amicable source upon which to open a conversation with the person he is witnessing to.

Chapter One, entitled, *The Origin of Religion*, sets the tone for understanding all major world religions. It enlightens the reader's understanding of the primitive religions as to their adherents' understanding of prayer, sacrificial ceremonies and their meaning, and their limited understanding and comprehension of the life after death. From this study, the reader will readily see the similarities of the major world religions as to their beliefs and forms of worship, tracing them all back to the primitive religions.

The reader will also note that in *Chapter Thirteen, Christianity*, he will see that because one calls one's self "Christian," it does not necessarily mean that one is a "Christian" in the true biblical sense of that word. One needs the saving grace of God through His Son, the Lord Jesus Christ in one's life to truly be a Christian.

Appendix "A" of this work gives the Christian witness a simple, yet logical Biblical sequence in the explanation of salvation and the leading of a person to Jesus Christ.

It is my sincere desire that this work may help the Christian witness to lead an adherent of one these world religions to a saving knowledge of the Lord Jesus Christ. If this is accomplished, this work has not been in vain.

CHAPTER ONE

The Origin of Religion

The word "Religious" comes from a Latin word meaning "to bind". Religion, therefore represents those activities which bind man to God in a certain relationship.[1] Religion may also be defined as man's attempt to achieve the highest good for his life by adjusting that life to the greatest power in the universe; that power usually being God.

Some religions are concerned with a belief. It is generally a belief in a god, gods, or supernatural being or beings, while other religions are concerned with a way or manner of living rather than believing. Most religions have defined systems of beliefs which are based on traditions and teachings. Religions can be compared with science in that as science seeks to discover facts and use them, religion seeks to discover values and to attract people to use and apply them through their worship and discipline.

What Religions Teach

All religions teach some form of ethics or codes of conduct, but religion goes even beyond this, for as ethics concerns itself with attitudes and behavior towards one another, religion is mainly concerned with people's relationship to God, (or whatever a particular religion's definition of "who is God?" or "what he might be").

Religion is a powerful force in the world. Men have died for their religious beliefs, either in the battlements of war or by persecution.

The Origin of Religion

After defining religion, the question may be asked, "From where and when did religion originate?" To answer this two-part question, it is necessary to look carefully into the definition of religion as previously stated. "Religion is mainly concerned with people's relationship to God." From where did religion originate? The only true answer that may be given in the light of the question asked, is that religion began in the Garden of Eden, where man's relationship to God was unspoiled (Genesis 1:26). The second part of the question which asks, "When did religion originate?" is open to much conjecture and debate, for the answer to this question depends on how one arrives at the date.

Some scholars do not reckon days in the context of the twenty-four hour period, but speak of generations and eons of times and ages, while others use the twenty-four hour day period. Even among these scholars there is much debate, not because of the time period but because of the reckoning of generations. One source dates Adam at about 4000 B.C.[2]

Why Are There So Many Religions?

I have dealt with only the major religions. If they are carefully studied, one may easily see that all sects and cults find their original roots in one of these major religions.

The answer to the above question lies in man's relationship to God, or better still, man's broken fellowship with God. Adam and Eve while in the state of innocence, had a perfect relationship to God, and their fellowship with Him was unbroken. When they sinned, that fellowship was broken (Genesis 3:1-26). Since that time, man has sought a way back to God. He has tried in many ways to communicate with God.

Some men have had or conceived revelations of how to return to full fellowship with God. They have called themselves God's elect, God's anointed, and God's prophets. They taught that only they had the true way back to God. Some of these holy men even placed themselves in a mediatorial position, stating that no one could come to God, but through them. The only true mediator between God and man is the Lord Jesus Christ (1 Timothy 2:5). How true is the fact that man has been and is incurably religious.[3]

Forms of Religion

Religion has taken on many forms and faces. Words such as "pantheism, " "animism," "polytheism" and "monotheism", have been used to describe many religions. Regardless of man's religion, as to how it began, it must be understood from the biblical standpoint that man is religious because God's intention was for man to have fellowship with Him as His child. Man was created by God for this purpose. His religious consciousness is a part of the divine image in which man is created.[4]

Primitive Religion

Primitive religion is also known as "animism", which means having a belief in spirits.[5] This is quite understandable, for man is, as well as being a being, a religious person, a spiritual person. He relates to, whether he admits it or not, a spiritual being. Primitive man has always believed in good and evil spirits. In the Christian religion one conceives good as coming from God, who is Spirit, and His angels, while evil proceeds from Satan and the fallen angels called demons. Primitive man, on the other hand, believed that spirits, good and evil, could possess inanimate objects such as stones, trees and even rivers. Therefore, he was careful in his approach to them, worshiping them with great sincerity.

Prayer in Religion

One of the oldest and most universal rites of religion is prayer.[6] Sacrifice closely followed it. Man, in his attempt to reach God, prayed. Today, man still prays. Sacrifices offered on his altars in order to have his sins expiated, were also made by man. Some of the very early tribal religions prayed in one form or another, but never offered sacrifices, while others blended the two together in their worship to God.

Prayer is the ladder between earth and heaven. Primitive religionists prayed for many things, spiritual and material. Men prayed before going into wars and battles. They prayed for power and peace and even spiritual revelations. Many of the primitive religions prayed to a "Great Spirit," while others prayed to many spirits and to inanimate objects of creation and to angels and holy men. To the Christian, prayer is indispensable. Through the prayer of faith, he receives

Christ as Savior, confesses his sin, worships God, receives healing for his body, communes with God and has fellowship with Him. Paul commanded all "to pray without ceasing" (1 Thessalonians 5: 17).

Prayer, in the primitive religions, included supplications and praises to God. Prayer is not to be equated with spell or magic. There is a fundamental difference. The latter was incorporated into some religions at a later date. This subsequently evolved into certain forms of religious worship such as "spiritism," "demonism" and even "Satanism".

The religious world outside of true Christianity has not changed much in the respect of worshiping demons, Satan, and the different forms of "spirit" worship. It is not just in the "Eastern countries" either. Among the intellectuals and the young college crowd, there is to be found worshipers of Satan, mediums who contact the spirit world and people who practice witchcraft. This is a far cry from even the primitive religions which ascended simple and sincere prayer to God.

The Word of God speaks loud and clear against such religious practices. It condemns these practices and declares God's wrath and judgment on all the practitioners of the occult (Exodus 22:18; Leviticus 19:31; 20: 6,27; and 1 Samuel 28:3,9). Paul encountered sorcery in his ministry and he dealt with it accordingly, (Acts 13:7-12; 16:16-24).

Sacrifices in Religion

Later primitive religions incorporated sacrificial rites into their worship. Animals and human life could be offered to the worshiper's god or gods for any number of reasons.

The general division of sacrifice applies in general to all primitive tribes. It can be stated as follows:

    I. Communal Sacrifice:
        A. A festive meal with or without a slain victim
        B. As pledge of kinship with the gods
   II. Honorific Sacrifice:
        A. Periodical gifts of honor to god
        B. Emergency gifts (for rain, etc.)
  III. Piacular Sacrifice for Propitiation:
        A. The gods as estranged or angry
        B. Blood sacrifice
        C. Hair offering (as part of victim)
        D. Salt covenant (salt = blood)[7]

The blood sacrifice was considered the highest of all sacrifices because it meant that the entire life was offered to God or a number of gods.

The Word of God alludes to the blood sacrifice in Genesis 3: 21. God instituted the Passover while the children of Israel were in Egypt (Exodus 12:1-51). These sacrifices pointed to the greater and nobler sacrifice of God's Son, Jesus Christ, who gave His sinless life for the sins of the world . Since the atoning death on the cross, all sacrifices cease for no more are necessary (Hebrews 9:1-28). However, it must be noted that Jesus must, of necessity, shed his Precious Blood for man's sins (Hebrews 9:22).

Fire-worship was one of the earliest forms of approach to the gods.[8] Egypt worshiped the Sun-god, Ra, and in India, Agni, the Fire-god, was given sincere worship by the faithful. The Chaldeans and the Phoenicians worshiped Baal who was a fire-god. The prophet Elijah encountered the prophets of Baal on Mount Carmel and there proved the futility of their worship to this pagan god (1 Kings 18:20-40).

Fire-worship and sun-worship are closely allied. In the ancient religions of Persia, India and China, the best examples of fire as a symbol of deity are found.

In the history of religion there seems to be only two genuine fire-gods. Hinduism has "Agni" and Zoroastrianism has "Atar". The Vestal virgins of Rome kept the eternal fires continually burning in the temple altars. Fire has been used by many cultures and religions as a method of communion with the divine. On some ancient religious altars, human as well as beastly offerings were made to the god or gods. They were consumed in fire to either appease the deity or deities or to gain favor or to give praise for favors received. Israel entered into such worship of pagan gods that resulted in God's wrath and judgment (2 Chronicles 28:3).

The Word of God speaks of fire. It connotes fire with purity. Many incidences are recorded concerning fire. The angel of the Lord appeared unto Moses in a flame of fire (Exodus 3:2). A chariot of fire and horses of fire were on the scene at Elijah's departing from the earth (2 Kings 2: 11). Isaiah had a hot coal of fire placed upon his mouth (Isaiah 6:7). These are only a few of the many instances when fire was used by God to prove His purity. How true Hebrews 12:29 is when it declares, "For our God is a consuming fire." First, came the " cloven tongues like as of fire," then proceeded the Holy Ghost to fill the very hearts and lives of the Christian believers in the upper room in Jerusalem.

They then went forth in holiness to win souls for their Lord and Savior, Jesus Christ.

The After-Life in Religion

Man, since his beginning, has believed in an existence after death. After the reader studies each religion, he will readily see this fact. This belief is universal among men. There are those who speak of life after death in terms of migration of the souls, while others talk of reincarnation. Each person hopes for a better life after death.

Man was created to live immortally. He sinned, and the consequence of that sin was death. The Scriptures speak of life after death. It speaks of heaven and hell, and so do other religious works. However, religions, other than Christianity, speak of a salvation by works to achieve immortality in a paradise setting, while Christianity speaks of eternity in heaven for the child of God in terms of faith in Jesus Christ as Savior. Works have no part in this salvation. Rejection of the Savior can only mean eternity in hell for the unbeliever at death. The story of Lazarus and the rich man is a classic example of this truth (Luke 16:19-31).

Time and space will not allow me to give a deep study to the doctrine of the resurrection. Man believes in the after –life. He strives to achieve the best possible life after death. Only Christianity, that is Jesus Christ, can guarantee life after death. His words are clear and plain when he says, "...I am the resurrection, and the life: he that believeth in me, though he were dead, yet shall he live: and whosoever liveth and believeth in me shall never die: Believest thou this?" (John 11: 25, 26).

There is no second chance after death in the biblical teaching; no purgatory or place of probation.

In studying the origin of religion, you will gain insight into the origins of prayer, sacrifice, fire-worship and fire as symbol of deity together with the origin of belief in immortality. This study will give you better insight into understanding each of the major religions discussed, and also how these religions differ from Christianity and the biblical understanding of the subjects covered in this chapter.

Notes

[1]Myer Pearlman, *Knowing the Doctrines of the Bible*, (Missouri: The Gospel Publishing House, 1937), p.8.

[2]Henry H. Halley, *Pocket Bible Handbook* (Chicago: Henry H. Halley Publisher, 1951), p.34.

[3]Samuel M. Zwemer, *The Origin of Religion*, (New York: Loizeaux Brothers, 1945), p.26.

[4]Luther E. Copeland, *Christianity and World Religions*, (Nashville: Broadman Press, 1963) p.4.

[5]Copeland, p.14.

[6]Zwemer, p.127.

[7]Zwemer, p.145

[8]Zwemer, p.153.

CHAPTER TWO

Confucianism

Origin and Founder

Confucianism the religion, and Confucius the founder, is synonymous. They cannot be separated. Confucius, one of eleven children, was born into a poor but respectable family. His place of birth was in the principality of Lu, China. He was then known as Chiu Kung. Later in life his disciples called him Kung Fu-tzu, meaning Kung, the Master. This was later latinized into Confucius.

From an early age, this man thirsted after knowledge. His desire was to see the people of his country better themselves morally and ethically, and by this means have a government that would exercise honest and truthful policies on behalf of its people. Because of this approach,

Confucianism is more philosophical and ethical in nature than it is religious.

Confucius was a humanitarian at heart. The central point of his thinking and teaching was expressed in one of his maxims, "What you do not want others to do to you, do not do to them." Centuries later, our blessed Lord declared, "Therefore all things, whatsoever ye would that men should do to you, do ye even so to them: for this is the law and the prophets (Matthew 7:12).

This great sage died at the age of seventy-three, a practical unknown to his people. Later, his sayings were collected by his disciples. This collection was later known as the "Analects."

Confucianisn became the state religion of China during the Ham Dynasty (206 B.C. – 220 A.D.). It remained so for over two thousand years until the Republic was established in 1912 A.D. During the Ham Dynasty, the worship of Confucius became official when the emperor in recognition of his teachings as supporting the imperial rule of China offered sacrifices at his tomb.

Though it was never his intention to be worshiped, this unknown philosopher, born into a poor family at a date uncertain (551— 479? B.C.), unrecognized by the majority of the vast population of his country during his life time commanded the adoration of more than 174 million people world-wide[1] until the Cultural Revolution of China.

Beliefs

Confucius believed in a Supreme Being — Shang Ti, to whom he prayed. He also believed in ancestor worship. He sacrificed to them and he encouraged others to do so.

He believed in the solidarity of the family. This belief gave reason for ancestor worship. Confucian philosophy emphasizes five basic relationships. Simply they are, (1) ruler and subjects; (2) father and son; (3) husband and wife; (4) older and younger brother; (5) friend and friend. Each of these specific relationships involves specific duties and manners. The Confucian mind rationalizes that if man will observe the duties and responsibilities of the five mentioned relationships, then he will realize heaven's pre-ordained harmony and justice.

Two major errors exist in the Confucian theology. Firstly, from the Christian stand-point, there is the error of ancestor worship. This entails the deification of man. The Word of God forbids this in the Ten Commandments which state, "Thou shalt have no other gods before me" (Exodus 20:3). Paul wrote to the Church at Rome, "As it is written, There is none righteous, no not one" (Romans 3:10). Further, to worship any human being, even Confucius, is to put that being in the place of Christ. Again, the Christian mind must reject this theology in light of New Testament teaching. The writer of the Acts of the Apostles is emphatic when he states, "Neither is there salvation in any other; for there is no other name under heaven given among men, whereby we must be saved" (Acts 4:12). The name of Jesus Christ is understood from verse 10.

It is evident from the Word of God that parenthood is to be respected, "Honor thy father and thy mother" (Matthew 19:19). However, to worship anyone or anything other than Christ is sure folly and damnation to the soul. Herein, we see the folly of the Confucian theology of worship.

Confucianism is to be admired for its teachings on ethical and moral matters, but again it strains its theology for it deceives its adherents into the false belief that through living morally and keeping the "golden rule," they can achieve salvation. Once again this teaching is at variance with Christian theology of salvation. Paul, in his letter to Titus, completely annihilates a doctrine of salvation by works. He writes, "Not by works of righteousness which we have done, but according to his mercy he saved us, by the washing of regeneration, and renewing of the Holy Ghost" (Titus 3:5).

Christians are commanded to do good works, not to attain or achieve salvation, but to give evidence of their salvation. This is made evident in Paul's letter to Titus as he writes, "In all things shewing thyself a pattern of good works: in doctrine shewing uncorruptness, gravity, sincerity," (Titus 2:7). Confucius' ethics are based on the wisdom of man rather than on a revelation from the living God.[2]

Confucius originally taught an ethical philosophy. This must be distinguished from the popular religion of the present day Chinese, which incorporates ancestor worship, animism, and involved social religions.[3]

Witness to a Confucist

A question may be asked, "In view of the Confucian theology of God and salvation, can an adherent to this religion be converted to Christianity?" The answer is, "Yes". Though deeply imbedded in the Confucian believer's mind is his theology, yet there is hope for him.

One must not over-simplify the matter. It is not as if one were witnessing to an occidental. The oriental mind must be taken into consideration together with Chinese customs as well.

Great care must be taken not to offend. Prayer and a knowledge of God's Word together with an understanding of the Confucian religion will greatly enhance the Christian believer's chance of witnessing successfully to the Confucian believer.

Patience and love are vital necessities in working with people of other religions, faiths and cultures. Faithful efforts in witnessing will bring fruitful results.

Notes

[1]*Information Please Almanac*, 1979 edition, p. 430.

[2]Kenneth Boa, *Cults, World Religions, and You.*, (Wheaton:Victor Books, 1978), p.40.

[3]Boa, p.40.

CHAPTER THREE

Taoism

Taoism ranks with Buddhism and Confucianism as the three great religions of China. Taoism is pronounced "Dowism." It is a mystical religion.

Founder

Lao Tzu (also "Lao Tse") was the supposed founder of Taoism. Some scholars doubt that he ever existed. He was, according to tradition, to have lived between 604 and 517 B.C. The name of this man means "Old Philosopher" or "Old Master." The sacred scriptures of Taoism are attributed to the authorship of Lao Tzu, but again there is speculation. These scriptures are called the "Tao Te Ching" which means "The Classic of the

Way and Its Power." Taoism received Imperial sanction in the 7th century A.D., as a recognized religion.

Origin

In its beginning, Taoism was a classical philosophical religion, but the common person could not understand its profound teachings. Consequently, it degenerated into a mystical, magical religion that had many gods, powers, and deified heroes. Its adherents practiced magic, sorcery and future telling.

Beliefs

Even in its inception, Taoism never believed in a personal Creator-God; only the Tao, which means "The Way". The very first chapter and verse of the book of Genesis gives the world a Personal-Creator God when it declares, "In the beginning God created the heaven and the earth."

When Taoism discusses "The Way," It refers to gentleness, economy and the shrinking from taking precedence of others. The Christian also has an understanding of "The Way", but "The Way" to him is a person and not an ideal. "The Way" is Jesus Christ who said, "I am the way, the truth and the life; no man cometh unto the Father, but by me." The virtues that Taoism advocates through "The Way," are what the Christian calls the "fruit of the Spirit." This fruit is love, joy, peace, longsuffering, gentleness, goodness, faith, meekness, temperance" (Galatians 5:22-23). This "fruit" may be the Christian's, only after he or she has been "born of the Holy Spirit" through a personal relationship with Jesus Christ, who is "The Way."

To the Taoist, the unseen world is possessed of good and evil spirits. All of nature is inhabited by these spirits. The evil spirits are dangerous; coming from the spirits of the dead.

This Chinese religion recognized a conflict within nature. The "Yin" stood for the earth, moon darkness, evil, and the female sex. On the other hand, there was the "Yang" which stood for heaven, the sun, light, fire, goodness, and the male sex. The evil spirits which are called "Yang" and the "Shen" which are the gods.

The only way one can be protected from the evil spirits is to worship many and varied gods or deities. Monks of the Buddhist faith together with the priest of the Taoist religion are employed to drive away the evil spirits. Thusly, witchcraft is used extensively in their rituals and ceremonies.

It was also thought that through the Tao, one could overcome the destructive forces of nature. The Tao hermits were believed to have concocted an elixir that when taken internally, would grant a person immortality, rendering a person immune from death.

The Word of God is diametrically opposed to any form of witchcraft, idolatry or astrology. It is satanic and can only cause damnation to the soul of the one who practices it. Paul, in his letter to the Galatians, calls witchcraft "a work of the flesh" (Galatians 5:19-21). Such practitioners in the Old Testament era were put to death (Exodus 22:18: Deuteronomy 18:10-12).

The Tao could not save anyone when it was a philosophical religion. How much less can it save after being relegated to a folk religion which practices divination and witchcraft?

The original Taoist beliefs are gaining the attention of the modern American. The folk religion Tao, with its evil practices, is being adhered to by millions of Americans under other names and disguises.

Witness to a Taoist

The Taoist must be brought to grips with his sin. Sin must be fully but simply explained to him, thus showing him that he is a sinner. "The Way" must be shown to him; "The Way " being Jesus Christ. One must be possessed of the Holy Spirit in His fullness and have a strong knowledge of God's Word, together, with a life of prayer to God for he will encounter in the true Taoist a life of demon possession.

A careful treatise will be given to the subjects of demonology and witchcraft in a separate chapter.

Bringing The Light Into The Darkness Of World Religions

CHAPTER FOUR

Hinduism

The religion of Hinduism is indefinable and indescribable. It has been said that it cannot be defined because it is "absolutely indefinite." It is described as being all-absorbing, all-tolerant, all-complacent, and all compliant:[1] A "Hindu" is an adherent of Hinduism.

Origin and Founder

No one can be a Hindu except by natural birth.[2] Scholars have traced this great religion, which is indigenous to India, to a beginning of about 2500 B.C. The word "Hindu" comes from the Persian word "Hind," which is the name for the Indus River region in northern India. The adherents of Hinduism are sometimes called

"Brahmanists" because of the influence of the Brahmains (priests) on the religion's growth. It may be noted at this point that Hinduism has no historical founder.

Out from this great religion have come other religions and sects. Notable of these are Buddhism, Jainism and Sikhism, which combined the beliefs of Hinduism with those of Islam. All these religions are dealt with in other chapters specific to them.

Beliefs

Nearly all the Hindu sects have retained the belief in karma and the transmigration of the soul. Brahma is the Supreme World-Soul or Spirit. He is the one absolute, infinite, indescribable, neuter Being. Actually, there is no human that can describe him, because humans are imperfect to do so. To the Hindu, Brahma is perfect and unchangeable.

Multitudes of gods are worshiped by the followers of Hinduism; but these gods are only a means to a more perfect understanding of Brahma. Three of these gods that are personifications of Brama, that are worshiped, are the Creator-Brahma; the Destroyer-Siva; and the Preserver or Renewer-Vishnu. Siva is the most worshiped of the gods because it is believed by his followers that as he destroys, he makes room for the new. Vishnu is considered to be the god of love. He has come to earth at other times and in other forms. Hindus worship these "avatars" or incarnations of him. Much honor is bestowed on Rama and Krishna who are considered two of Vishnu's greatest incarnations. Many of the followers of Hinduism now consider Brahma quite unimportant because he has fulfilled his task as Creator.

The followers of this great religion have been taught that the essence of all living things is "atman" — its spirit or soul which proceeds from Brahma. Therefore, it is reasoned that because every animal has a soul, they should be respected but not worshiped. This is the reason why animals are not killed for food. The cow is a sacred figure as it symbolizes man's identity with life.

The ultimate desire and goal of man's life and soul is to be united with Brahma. However, to achieve this bliss, more than one lifetime will have to be lived.

Reincarnation or transmigration of the soul is one of the teachings of this religion. It is believed that the soul is not born, therefore, it does not die. It just passes from one body to another until it is pure enough to be reunited with Brahma. The law of "karma" (the law of cause and effect), which is also called the law of deed, regulates the movements of the soul. This law in effect, means that the deeds of a person in one life determines the next life that he will lead. Karma will not be in operation when a follower's soul achieves union with Brahma. The soul is then released from the cycles of life and death. Man can become one with Brahma if proper discipline of the mind and body is maintained. This discipline is called "yoga" and today it is practiced by millions of Americans.

One of the sacred scriptures: the "Bhagavad-Gita" gives three ways of teaching Brahma. The first concerns the performance of good works or deeds. The second concerns thought, philosophy and meditation, and the third way is the way to devotion and faith to one god. The last way is considered to be the best.

The subjects of karma and reincarnation are dealt with in chapters on the three other religions that came out of Hinduism, which were Sikhism, Buddhism and Jainism. However, I would like to add some information and insight into these two subjects.

Firstly, karma has no biblical basis for its belief. Because the latter part of Galatians 6:7 reads, "...for whatsoever a man soweth, that shall he also reap," it is not to be taken that the actions of this life will determine the state of the next life. The cultists who extract this doctrine from Hinduism and try to equate it with biblical teaching, are only being satanically led to deceive people. This idea is refuted by Christ when He explained that the man who was blind from birth was not born so because of personal sins that he committed in this life or any previously.

Paul rightfully cleared up any misunderstanding on this point when he wrote to the church at Corinth. He stated, "Therefore, if any man be in Christ, he is a new creature; old things are passed away: behold, all things are become new" (2 Corinthians 5:17).[3]

The subject of reincarnation needs to be addressed at this point. Because Jesus referred to John the Baptist as Elijah, the cultists of the "Eastern mystical thought," take this to mean that Jesus taught reincarnation. St. Luke clarified this difficulty when he writes that John came "In the spirit and power of Elijah" (Luke 1:17). The transfiguration account of Matthew 17 also refutes this false teaching. John the Baptist was asked, "Are you Elijah?" He firmly answered, "I am not" (John 1:21).

The Bible is concerned with the doctrine of the resurrection of Christ and His followers and not the idea of any reincarnation. The Christian will have a glorified body; not a tormented soul that may never achieve a state of perfection.[4]

Stated briefly, "yoga means "union." It comes out of the branch of Hinduism known as "Philosophical Hinduism." Yoga is performed to suppress bodily activity and breathing. Mental activity is also suppressed in order for the person to come into a blissful state of serene contemplation with Brahma. A person who practices yoga is called a "yogi," or yogin." The "Upanshids" are the sacred writing of "Yoga."

Sin and moral guilt are not recognized by the followers of Hinduism. It is a religion of works; therefore, there is no need for forgiveness. Salvation may be achieved through many births and many lives. Hinduism denies the claims of Christ. As a matter of fact, it despises His teachings and the Christian teaching that Christ is the only way to God.[5]

There are two dominant types of Hinduism. There is the "Popular Hinduism" and the "Philosophical Hinduism."[6] "Popular Hinduism" is for the masses. It covers the observance of the caste system, the worship of the idols of the many popular gods, which is attended with rites and ceremonies that are steeped in superstition, and the fables and folk stories of the gods.

The caste system began as a hereditary social order and ended up in the religious teachings of Hinduism. There are four traditional castes.

The first includes the intellectuals and the Brahma or the priests. The second is the "Kshatriya's" who are the warriors and the rulers. Thirdly, there is the "Vaisyas," casts known as the "Sudras" which are the unskilled laborers. The "Pariah's" are the "untouchables" which belong to no class at all. India outlawed "untouchables" in 1947.

Hindus were taught that one was in a certain caste because of the previous life, but could be in a higher caste if the deeds were good only after a re-birth. One caste was forbidden to have any social or religious association with one another. Today there are more than 3,000 sub-castes.

The Christian gospel teaches that the re-birth takes place in this world when one genuinely accepts Jesus Christ as one's own personal Lord and Savior (John 3:1-21). Furthermore, Christ never taught a caste-system doctrine. He ate with publicans and sinners. He healed lepers, and cast out demons. He preached to the hated Samaritans. Our blessed Lord touched every class of people in His lifetime and even today His gospel is extended to all who will believe it.

Philosophical Hinduism is very mystical. Cutting through much of the history attending this type of Hinduism, one can see simply and clearly that God is neuter and not personal. He is called "Brahma." He is without qualities and is unknowable. One must speak of God as "It" and not "He" because "He" is impersonal. "It" is "Reality," the "Unchangeable One". In the positive sense, "It" is spoken of as absolute existence, consciousness and bliss. Negatively, "It" cannot be comprehended mentally; it is quality-less, causeless, energy-less, indescribable, limitless, above good and evil, personality and gender, distinction and difference. With all of this, the Hindus speak of the Brahma and assign attributes to that which is attribute-less.[7] The "Yoga" which was discussed earlier in this chapter comes under this major type of Hindusim.

Christianity takes a totally opposite view of God. It talks of God, as being a Person. The book of Genesis states, "And God said, Let us make man in our likeness" (Genesis 3:26). This book also states, "So God created man in his own image, in the image of God created he him; male and female created he them" (Genesis 1:27). The Gospel of John concurs with that of the book of Genesis when it says, "In the beginning was the Word, and the Word was with God, and the Word was God. The same was in the beginning with God. All things were made by him; and without him was nothing made that was made. In him was life; and the life was the light of men" (John 1:1-4). This is not understandable by the followers of Hinduism or any other religion, as the Word of God makes very clear. John clearly elucidates this fact when under the inspiration of the Holy Spirit he writes, "And the light shineth in darkness; and the darkness comprehended it not" (John 1:5).

The darkness in the world, where every heart is darkened by sin, remain ignorant, degraded and unholy, and earlier revelations to men proved insufficient.[8] Men's revelations, if they do not align with the revelation of God's Word, will always be false. To build a doctrinal system upon a false premise will make all other doctrines false. One must begin with the God of Genesis as a Person and continue with Him throughout the entire Word of God with Him as a Person and not an abstract being or principle.

At this point in the discussion, it would be well to point out the various scriptures of this religion. These scriptures were written during the various periods and phases of its growth.

There were the "Four Vedas" (around 1000 B..C.), which represent the period of early nature worship. The "Brahmas" (from about 800 to 600 B.C.) covers the priestly Hinduism. The "Upanishads" (around 600 to 300 B.C.) concerns the philosophic Hinduism. The "Laws of Manu" (around 250 B.C.) deal with the legalistic Hinduism. The "Bhagavad-Gita" (around 1 A.D.) represent devotional Hinduism. Finally, there are the "Epics and Puranas" (200 B.C. to ? A.D.) which deal with popular Hinduism. The doctrines and traditions taught and propagated in these various sacred works are discussed in this book.

Witness to a Hindu

Patience, love and prayer by a dedicated, Spirit-filled Christian can win a disciple of the Hindu faith to Christ. Christ must be exalted (John 12:32). Man must be stripped of his "deity" as so believed by the Hindu believers. God must be made known as a Person and not as a principle. Sin must be shown as man's downfall. This seems so very difficult at first, but God will reveal Himself as the Christian witness unfolds His Word with love and patience.

Various forms of Hinduism (especially the Vedantic ideas), have become popular with the American youth. It is spreading on college campuses throughout our nation. Christian witnesses are needed not only to win the Hindu's to Christ, but to also win the youth of our country from such insidious beliefs which can only harm and damn the soul.

I have given much time to this religion because it gave birth to three other major religions which are influencing America in its views, ideas and doctrines, and in turn, giving birth to many cults. These cults come forth with their so-called revelators who have received a specific and original revelation from God, when in truth, they have just propagated some ungodly idea from Hinduism. To understand Hinduism, therefore, is to understand many of these mystical beliefs being paraded before the American people.

They can be stopped. How? By intercessory prayer, studying the Word of God, and knowing the plan of salvation and how to present it.

Notes

[1]Copeland, p.27.

[2]Howard F.Vos, *Religions in a Changing World* (Chicago: Moody Press, 1966), p.189.

[3]Pat Means, *The Mystical Maze,*(San Bernardion: Campus Crusade For Christ, Inc., 1976), p.103.

[4]Means, pp.103-104.

[5]Boa., p.17.

[6]Vos, p.194.

[7]Vos., p.197.

[8]George W. Clark and J. M. Pendleton, *The New Testament With Brief Notes,* (Chicago: The Judson Press, 1949), p.238.

CHAPTER FIVE

Buddhism

Origin

Buddhism, like Jainism, began as a reformation movement within the religion of Hinduism.
Siddhartha Gautama was its founder. Many leg-
ends and myths are attached to his birth and early
childhood. The probable date of his birth was
around 560 B.C. He died at the age of 80 from
either food poisoning or indigestion.

Founder

Gautama, at the age of twenty-nine, left his
family and a life of great luxury and wealth to
find inner peace and salvation. After much
searching and self-mortification he found Nirvana
(the freeing of the soul from all that enslaves it),

while sitting under a tree. At that time he became the "Buddha," or the "Enlightened" or
"Awakened One."

Beliefs

Buddhism, in the original state, had no god
to worship. Buddha retained two major thoughts
from Hinduism; the endless cycle of rebirths
(Samsara), and the law of cause and effect
(karma). Karma means the force generated by a
person's actions to perpetuate transmigration and
to determine his destiny in his next existence. As
with all philosophical religions, Buddhism leaves
a person with no hope for the present and no hope
for the future.

Gautama Buddha's doctrines were simple.
They began with four fundamental truths which
he called the "Four Noble Truths." They were (1)
The noble truth of suffering; (2) The noble truth
of the cause of suffering, (The cause for his suffering concerned desire; desire for pleasure; the
desire for existence and the desire for prosper-
ity); (3) The noble truth concerned with the cessation of suffering; that is to eradicate the desire, and the suffering ceases; (4) The noble truth
of the path that leads to the cessation of suffering, which is the eightfold path (middle path) that
consists of (a) right views; (b) right aspirations;

(c) right conduct; which includes no killing, stealing, lying, adultery, and drinking intoxicants; (d) right livelihood; (e) right endeavor; (f) right awareness; and (g) right meditation.

Each convert to Buddha must take the oath of the "Three Refuges." Which are (1) I take refuge in the Buddha; (2) I take refuge in the doctrine; and (3) I take refuge in the order.

There are five other precepts that are held on certain holy days , and which are held by some monasteries throughout the year. These precepts are (1) not to eat at forbidden times; (2) not to dance, listen to music, or to attend theatrical plays; (3) not to use cosmetics or wear jewelry for personal adornment; (4) not to use a high bed; (5) not to receive silver or gold.

The Buddhist's goal is "nirvana," and this in the original concept of Gautama's thinking. This can become quite complicated, however, it may be explained in the following way. The concept of "nirvana" is the extinction of all desire and the complete and final release from all suffering. A number of rebirths may be needed to accomplish the "nirvana." If a person is not good in this lifetime, that person may be born on a lower scale in the next birth.

In the quest of "nirvana," there are five mental hazards which must be overcome and ten fetters which must be broken away from. The five mental hazards are (1) sensual desire; (2) ill-will; (3) sloth and torpor; (4) agitation and worry; and (5) doubt. The ten fetters are as follows; (1) belief in a self; (2) uncertainty; (3) belief in the efficacy of good works; (4) evil thirst; (5) evil attitudes; (6) desire to live on earth; (7) desire for future life in heaven; (8) pride; (9) self-righteousness; and (10) ignorance.

To understand Buddhism in its present state it must be viewed through two main branches. Southern Buddhism which is called "Hinayna" or "the lesser vehicle," is the original or orthodox branch. It stays very closely to Gautama's teachings.

The "Mahayana" branch of Buddhism deifies Buddha, even though he never claimed divinity. He never even claimed that there was a god. "Mahayana" would even dare to claim that Buddha was never human. The way of salvation of this branch of religion is the repeating of the names of the "Bodhisattavas" who were those who could have attained "nirvana" but abstained in order to help others obtain it. The lotus flower became the emblem of "The Mahayana" branch of Buddhism. They also believe in a heaven and a hell. Images were introduced to help the illiterate understand the religion. Gautama's original theism was supplanted by an idolatrous polytheistic belief.

From one extreme of the spectrum of atheistic belief to the polytheistic belief, leaves Buddhism an ungodly religion that gives no hope of salvation to its believers, yet millions follow it with tenacious desire. Zen Buddhism, which came out of Japan, and which has become very popular in America, believes that salvation can only be achieved through a person's self. The Zen Buddhist believes that truth can only be realized and experienced through intuitive wisdom by means of meditation.

Zen holds the view that there is no god outside the universe who has created it or man. Zen appeals to the western mind in that it completely removes the need for any dogma or doctrine. The issue of salvation is within the being of man's self and how man deals with the problem salvation within that self. Man, therefore, does not have to reckon with or give an account to an outside force called god or whatever. The real appeal of Zen to the modern mind is a "flight from God through enlightenment."[1]

Buddhism has manifold sects which hold their own conception of god (or not of god), and of the way of salvation.[2]

Buddhism has no form that has a place for the biblical doctrines of God, man, sin, salvation or resurrection. The sect's views are either polytheistic, pantheistic or atheistic.[3]

One form of Buddhism does what many cults of the modern day do; that is, use terms similar to those used in the Christian faith; such terms as "the new birth," "salvation by faith" and "changed lives." This form of Buddhism, which is called "Amida Buddhism' never comes to grips with the problem of sin.

Gautama Buddha had set many great moral standards for his subjects to adhere to, and they are to be admired. I do not feel led to take each standard and compare it with Christian moral standards, as both religions agree on many of these standards. However, I make this one great distinction between the two religions; that being, the existence of God; that He is creator of the universe and man; that He alone should be worshiped, and that worship should be through His Son, the Lord Jesus Christ, and finally, the problem of sin must be dealt with. These facts leave Buddhism and Christianity worlds apart, and never the twain shall meet because the former leaves out the person of the Lord Jesus Christ. The Buddhist must be shown these distinctions if he is ever to realize his error. This will take the prayerful work of a Spirit-filled Christian who has knowledge of Buddhism and the Word of God.

Witness to a Buddhist

The Christian witness must be friendly to the Buddhist believer. There must be a good rapport. One thing is most important and that is not to approach the Buddhist with negative thoughts and remarks about his religion, but to remark on the good aspects of his religion, yet not with too great an emphasis, lest he think there is no difference between the two religions. Be conversational and not "preachy."

The Christian uses words totally foreign to the religious mind of the Buddhist; words such as love, God, and sin. These words will have to be explained with much care and patience. A book titled, *Religions in a Changing World*, has a special chapter on Buddhism and gives important and detailed information on how a Christian should witness to a Buddhist.[4]

A Buddhist can be won to Christ by presenting Christ in a Christ-like manner. As our Lord reached the "woman at the well," so must the Christian reach the Buddhist (John 4:1-30).

Notes

[1]Copeland, p.60.
[2]Boa., p.30.
[3]Boa., p.30..
[4]Vos., pp.179-186.

CHAPTER SIX

Sikhism

Origin

Sikhism began in India in the 1500's A.D. This was around the same time that the Protestant Reformation began in Europe.

Founder

The founder of this religion was Guru Nanak who lived from 1469 to 1538 A.D. He was born the son of a village accountant in Talvandi, India, which is some 30 miles from the city of Lahore. He died at Kartarpur, India, in 1538 A.D.

Guru Nanak was influenced by holy men; some of whom represented the Hindu Bhakti school, while others represented the Sufi form of Islam. Nanak called his God, "Sat Nam" or True

Name." To him, this God was a loving teacher or "Guru" which means "Teacher."

Nanak's primary intention was to unite the Moslems and all castes (classes of Hindus) into one "Brotherhood." He stated that there was no Hindu and there was no Muslim. His desire was to remove ritualism, ceremonialism, self-mortification and pilgrimages from the religions. The Guru Nanak had a simple religion. To be saved, one had only to meditate upon and repeat the name of "Sat Nam," yet beneath this simplicity there was a more intricate system that was used for obtaining salvation. This system combined works and grace.

Beliefs

The conception of God in this religion is that He is formless, sovereign, unknowable, absolute, yet His grace can be called upon. The Sikhs developed a monotheism that was abstract and mystical, bordering on pantheism. When, or if man reaches a place of salvation, that man is absorbed into God. As this religion is a syncretism of Islam and Hinduism, this idea is from the Hinduistic teaching. Total submission to God is from the Islamic concept of salvation.

Sikhism turned from a pacifist religion to one of militarism because of the Moslem persecution.

The "Adi Grath" became the sacred scriptures of Sikhism. They worshiped this book even though many could not read or understand it because of the various languages it was written in.

Sikhism today, is like many other religions. Its adherents are mechanical in their worship. The present day Sikh observes a few of the special days and ceremonies such as initiation, baptism, marriage and funerals.

As with followers of any other religious belief, Sikhs can be converted to Christianity. The beliefs contained in this religion are being fused into modern day mystical religious groups that incorporate Sikh beliefs with those of other religions and propagate and promote them as a new revelation from God.

Sikhism seems to be a dying religion. However, Islam is thriving and Hinduism is still a major world religion. Sikhism tried to blend these two world religions into one, seeking to take the best teachings from each. Based on the above statements, I conclude that one need not fear this religion under its beliefs.

Belief in one "God" is held by Judaism (Deuteronomy 6:4). Christians also hold tenaciously to this view of God. However, to hold to this view that upon being saved, one must have been totally absorbed into God, leaves one open to pantheism.

A mingling of God's grace with works to achieve salvation is typical of many religions as well as Sikhism. This subject has been dealt with previously in the author's discussion on other religions.

Witness to Sikh

Christians must focus on the person of the Lord Jesus Christ, His atoning work on the cross, His substitutionary death and ultimate resurrection, in order to penetrate the mind of a Sikh.

Karma and the transmigration of souls will be carefully studied under the Hindu religion.

CHAPTER SEVEN

Jainism

Origin

The religion of Jainism is indigenous to India. It is almost nonexistent outside that great country. The word "Jain" means "victor." Some accept this religion on its own merits while others insist that it is nothing more than a sect within the larger religion of Hindusim. Nevertheless, it has certain doctrinal distinctives which will be discussed later.

Founder

Nataputta Vardhamana, better known by his title, "Mahavira," which means, "Great Man," founded this religion. He lived from 599 B.C. to 527 B.C. He was born into a family of ruling caste, which afforded him all the luxuries of that day. Unhappy and restless with this way of life, Mahavira sought for a truth that would satisfy his inner man and grant him peace of mind and salvation.

According to the Jain scriptures, he tortured his body and mind with fastings, exposing himself to the severe cold of winter and heat of summer in an attempt at self-mortification, in order to find salvation. His quest was not in vain. He found enlightenment. From that point in time in his life, he began preaching and acquiring a following of disciples.

Beliefs

To become a "Jina," the Jain has achieved his goal, for he has become a "victor," as did the Mahavira before him. At that point in his life, he has been delivered from the cycle of re-birth. The Jain, it must be remembered, is atheistic in his religion in that he denies the existence of a Supreme Being or Creator: therefore, his salvation is humanistic.[1]

To the Jain, the universe is uncreated and eternal. This leaves him to believe that man must rely on his own resources. He never looks to outside forces for help, this is foolish to him He can only be relieved from suffering and escape from rebirth by severe self-discipline and asceticism.[2]

There are three "Jewels" in the religion of Jainism. They are right knowledge, right faith, and right conduct. They will kill no living matter; not even injure it if possible.

The Jains believe that all plants, insects, fire, water, wind and earth, possess living souls.[3] The true Jain vows non-injury to living things, speaking the truth, not to steal, sexual abstinence and non-attachment. This rigorous method is faithfully followed in order to counteract the bad "karma" with good and liberate them, thus giving them eternal bliss. This is self-salvation. "Karma" is the material that keep the soul in bondage.

Jainism offers its adherents no hope. It gives God no place in its egocentric religion. Man works out his salvation but is never sure of achieving or securing it. He may have to go through many rebirths and still never find peace of mind, happiness or salvation.

Jainism's doctrinal errors are, to say the least, to be despised by all Christian standards. This religion denies God His role as Creator of the universe; even His existence. The Holy Bible totally rejects this belief in the opening statement of the book of Genesis that says, "In the beginning God created the heaven and the earth" (Genesis 1:1). Dr. C.I. Scofield succinctly states, "The Bible begins with God, not with philosophic arguments for this existence."[4] This may not only apply to the followers of Jainism but also all religionists who deny the existence of God as the Supreme Being and Creator of the universe.

Jainism uses the word "soul" when it speaks of human life, animal life, and certain non-living matter such as water and fire. It would be wise at this point to briefly discuss the meaning of "soul" in the light of the Word of God and what the Christian concept of it is. The soul distinguishes the life of man and beast from inanimate things, (fire, water, etc.), and also from the unconscious life like that of plants. [5]

Both man and beast have souls (Genesis 1: 20). And from this scriptural text, it is learned that the word "life" is "soul" in the original. This is referred to as conscious soul. Man's soul distinguishes him from animals. They have a soul, but it lives only as long as the body lasts (Ecclesiastes 3:21). Man's soul differs in that it is quickened by a human spirit. Man lives by reason; animals by their instincts.[6]

Because man lives by reason and has a rational mind, he must give an account of his deeds. He is responsible for his actions. Since he sinned at Eden (Genesis 3:1-24), he no longer lives a life of innocence. He takes on the sin nature of Adam and because of this, he needs atonement for his sin. This atonement comes only through the Lord Jesus Christ. (1 Corinthians 15:22).

Herein does Jainism err concerning its understanding of the word "soul." Jainism speaks of many "re-births" in order to free the soul. This thinking opens the door to the doctrine of "reincarnation," which has no place in Christian theology. The only "re-birth" the Christian mind understands is that of the "born-again experience as explained by Jesus to Nicodemus (John 3:1-15). The Christian view of the re-birth is totally different to the view of many re-births of Jainism.

Concerning the doctrine of salvation by works which the converts to Jainism adhere to, *Chapter Two, Confucianism* discusses this point at some length.

Jainism, as a religion that wishes to dispose of the caste system, free the soul to live in peace, and grant salvation through works, must be considered a social and spiritual failure.[7]

One may never meet a believer of this religion in America, but two important things must be kept in mind. Firstly, one may be called to India as a missionary and the knowledge given here may help to understand the religion and give impetus to further study. Secondly, many of the doctrines of this ancient oriental religion are given under the guise of a new religion by leaders of sects in this country who wish for a following. It is hoped that the information imparted in this chapter may open the eyes of people to fallacy of such a sect and to the consequences that it could have in terms of eternity.

Witness to a Jainist

Jainists believe in sin. The Christian may use the subject of sin as the focal point of his discussion with a believer in Jainism and through the Word of God, and with the help of the Holy Spirit, a believer can lead a Jainist to a genuine faith in Christianity.

Notes

[1]Boa, p.10.
[2]Boa, p.19.
[3]Boa, p.19.
[4]*The Holy Bible, New Scofield Reference Edition*, p.1.
[5]Pearlman, p.104
[6]Pearlman, p.104.
[7]Boa, p.20.

CHAPTER EIGHT

Shintoism

Origin and Founder

The religion of Shinto is indigenous to Japan. However, because of the Japanese population that is concentrated on our west coast, this religion must be understood by the Christian in order to witness to the American Japanese people.

This religion has no founder and its origin is obscure. It has been passed down through the centuries by word of mouth, tradition, and through certain religious rites and practices which keep it alive.

Two Chinese words, shen (spirit) and tao (the way), in combination, produce the word Shinto. The Japanese equivalent is "kami no michi," which means "the way of the gods."

Beliefs

Shintoism is a very primitive and undeveloped religion. It centers on nature deities and deified people. There is no savior in this religion and it boasts of no certain or special doctrine. Shintoism is pantheistic in nature in that it makes no clear distinction between the creator and the created.[1] The shrine is the center of Shinto worship, for there the Shintoist believes that deities dwell there.

The Shinto religion, sad to say, offers no hope of salvation to anyone, for it promises none to anyone. Its only promise is that a Japanese will remain Japanese forever.[2]

Religion in Japan is a matter of custom and decree rather than conviction. It has no conviction in it such as Christianity has, therefore, the followers of this religion have a vague idea about its beliefs. The gods of this religion have no morals or ethics.[3] The Confucian influence in Shintoism raised its standards of conduct and culture, while the Buddhist influence brought a deeper thought into it.

Shintoism has one main thrust; to distill patriotism into the Japanese people. This was very evident in World War II when the Japanese people thought of their emperor as a god and deified him.

The Shinto is steeped in Ancestor worship. This could have been because of the Chinese influence. The Japanese believe that they are of a divine origin. This makes them good. If they appease the gods and do their bidding, they are saved. There is no sin because of this divine origin.

Shintoism can become very complex with its three main sects, and the influence that Buddhism has had upon it as well as that of Confucianism. I have endeavored to bring out the main points of this religion. To be able to refute just one idea or principle of this religion, which is alien to the Christian thought, will show its fallacy and thereby prove that its beliefs are a damnation to the soul.

Shintoism, like Confucianism and many other similar religions, because it gives no place to Christ in its teaching, is worthless. Jesus declared that He was the Beginning and the End (Revelation 21:6; 22:13). Whatever morals it teaches or practical ethics it advances may be found in other religions.

Again we are faced with the dilemma of many gods, or a polytheistic worship. The Ten Commandments at once nullify this doctrine (Exodus 20:1-17). The idea of Ancestor worship is also brought to nought by the Word of God.

Witness to a Shinto

Can a Shintoist, who feels he has found the "way," be converted to Christianity? The answer is "yes."

The Christian must emphatically stress the doctrine of the resurrection of Jesus Christ. This victorious and supernatural event will appeal to the Shintoist mind. Again, be encouraged that the power of the Holy Spirit will give the Christian witness the wisdom and understanding he needs in dealing with the Shinto adherents.

Notes

[1]Boa, p.45.
[2]Vos, p.92.
[3]Vos, p.93.

CHAPTER NINE

Islam

Origin and Founder

Ubu'l Kassim was born in Mecca, in 570 A.D. He is known to the present day world as Mohammed, founder of the religion of "Islam," which means "submission to God." At the age of forty he had a vision in which he was instructed by an angel what his task was and that he was the prophet of Allah (meaning God).

Mohammed was born and raised around people who were polytheistic. They not only worshiped Allah but many other gods. Mohammed hated this form of worship. He tenaciously held to the view of One True Living God whose name was "Allah," and he (Mohammed) was his prophet.

The prophet Mohammed's first convert was his wife. He experienced much persecution in

Mecca because of his religious persuasion. Consequently, he and his followers took flight to Medina that was also in Arabia. This flight, known as the "Hegira," which took place in 622 A.D. was most important to the Moslems. Their calendar dates from it.

Beliefs

Mohammedanism has its fundamental beliefs as do many of the world religions. Because Mohammed was influenced by the Jewish and Christian religions, various doctrines of these religions have been woven into the doctrinal fabric of Islam. Mohammed's misunderstanding of these doctrines, clearly reveals a misconception of the person of God; of Jesus Christ; and of the Holy Trinity. The Koran is unreliable in stating its views on the above mentioned doctrines.

It is a difficult task to discuss the religion of Islam analytically, because it carries such a broad range of doctrines and traditions. However, I will endeavor to cover a few of its beliefs and compare them with the Word of God.

There are six fundamental beliefs in the Moslem faith. The first of these is the belief in God, (Allah). Though revered and worshiped by the Moslems, Allah, as they call God, is unknowable. He is prayed to religiously, but the prayers are mostly mechanical; having no spiritual value in them. The Christian, on the other hand, finds solace and comfort in prayer. He expects God to hear and answer his prayers. He received Christ as Savior by praying (Romans 10:13). He calls on God for personal needs, and God answers to those needs (James 1:5; 5:14). He prays for the needs of others, and God is ready to supply those needs (Philemon 4; 2 Thessalonians 1:11,12). The disciples of Jesus were aware of not only the value of prayer in their personal lives, but also the proper method of prayer. They asked Him to teach them to pray, and He responded with the magnificent prayer found in Saint Luke's gospel, 11: 1-4. Jesus' personal life was one of profound intercessory prayer (Mark 14: 36-39), as should all true Christian's prayers (1 Thessalonians 5:17). In praying, there should be a heart of thanksgiving to God for answered prayer (Psalm 135:3; 1 Thessalonians 5:18).

Because the Moslem has no knowledge of God, his prayers are not only mechanical, but they also are repetitious (Matthew 6:7). God can be known, but only through the person of the living Christ (John 14:10).

The religion of Islam is to be admired for its monotheistic belief, but it fails in its understanding of God in that it does not understand God. Suffice to say, the author could end his treatise here, but his purpose is to show the beliefs of the

Moslem religion and how they differ from Christianity, and in so differing, fall short in bringing a convert into a personal relationship with God that will endure through the eternities.

The second belief of the Moslem religion concerns "Predestination." To the Moslem, God is absolute sovereign over all. Everything is attributed to His divine will. Human freedom plays a very minor role in Islamic thought. Godfrey E. Phillips says of Islam, "Man has no heavenly Father, but a heavenly Sultan, and must behave accordingly."[1]

The Word of God shows that the divine sequence is foreknowledge, election, and predestination. Election is according to God's foreknowledge, and predestination is the fulfilling of that election (1 Peter 1:2). Salvation is not affected by foreknowledge, election, or predestination, as John 3: 16 most assuredly points out. Man who believes in Christ is saved. This shows the measure of God's grace, and the free will of man in accepting God's grace.[2]

Islam leaves out one of the attributes that is essential to God; that is love, (1 John 4:8). Because of His love, God shows grace and mercy to the penitent heart. The Islamic doctrine of "Kismet" or fate, pervades the entire life of the Moslem. His thinking is absorbed with it, and he does not take precaution in his daily living habits.

The third belief of the Moslem faith is that of believing in angels. The Moslem understanding of angels and some of their functions comes near the Judaic and Christian concepts. Angels play an important role in the work of the Lord. They were God's messengers to the Old Testament prophets. They proclaimed the birth of the Lord Jesus Christ (Luke 1: 26-37; 2:9-14)). They ministered to Christ after his temptation by Satan (Matthew 4:11). Angels are inferior to Christ. They are appointed to serve the subjects of His grace who are destined to inherit through His eternal salvation. [3]

The fourth fundamental belief is that of the belief in prophets or apostles. As can well be understood, Mohammed is the chief prophet. The remaining prophets or apostles are men who Allah has chosen to receive His revelation that has come through His angels. These prophets are to proclaim that message. Mohammed accepted a number of the prophets of the Old Testament; among them were Noah, Abraham and Moses. Jesus was also accepted. Mohammed, however, received the full and complete revelation.

Prophets had their place in the work of the Lord. God revealed His Word to them, and in obedience to His divine will they wrote the Word of God that will be a living testament for eternity. Peter declares this fact when he writes, "For the prophecy came not in old time by the will of man; but holy men of God spake as they were moved by the Holy Ghost" (2 Peter 1:21). The apostle Paul, in his letter to the Hebrews, also makes note of this fact but he adds, "Hath in these last days spoken unto us by (in) His Son, whom he hath appointed heir of all things, by whom He also made the worlds" (Hebrews 1:2). Therefore, Jesus Christ is the final authority. No new revelation has been given to Mohammed or any other prophet since the time of Christ. As Christ is superior to Moses and the angels, so is He superior to Mohammed (Hebrews 1:6; 3:1-6). Jesus Christ is the Son of God, and God the Son. Thomas said of the blessed Lord, "—My Lord and my God" (John 20:28).

Mohammed could not understand the deity of Christ, neither could he accept the Christian and scriptural concept of the "Holy Trinity." Moslems today think of the "Holy Trinity" as being "God, Mary and Jesus." This Christian doctrine is hated by the Moslem because they believe that it destroys the divine unity.[4]

To give a qualified exegesis on the subject of the "Holy Spirit" would entail much time and labor and space. I suggest that a simple doctrinal book be acquired and studied on this subject. To witness to the Moslem, the Christian should present Christ, His death on the cross and His resurrection. The Holy Spirit will guide the Christian witness, and the truth of the gospel of Christ will find a lodging place in the heart of the Moslem believer.

The fifth basic belief of the Moslems is in the scriptures. Mohammed was the final prophet. He was given the final revelation. That revelation is in the Koran, therefore, Islam looks to no other authority than the Koran. It is their "Word."

Other books considered sacred, but lesser in importance than the Koran, are the Tauret (The Pentateuch) of Moses, the Zabur (Psalms) of David and the Injil (Evangel) of Jesus. However, in the Moslem mind, as Allah is eternal, so is the Koran.

The Christian believes that the Holy Bible with its sixty-six canonical books contain the complete divine revelation of redemption. It is inerrant. The Word of God is inspired of God as succinctly stated by Peter (2 Peter 1:21). The Holy Bible lives, because Christ lives. He is the living Word (John 1:1-5). As a matter of fact, the Word of God does not give mention to Mohammed as a prophet. It does not foretell of his coming, and that he will be the greatest prophet. It does state however, in Jesus' own words, "Verily I say unto you, Among them that are born of women there hath not risen a greater than John the Baptist; notwithstanding he that is least in the kingdom of heaven is greater than he" (Matthew 11:11). John himself, showing the true signs of a prophet, said concerning Christ, "He must increase, but I must decrease" (John 3:30). We may therefore conclude that the Holy Bible, which is also rightly called the Word of God, is all sufficient in meeting man's spiritual need.

The sixth and last belief of the Moslem is his belief in the "last day." This concerns the resurrection and judgment, and the world to come. Believers have their place in paradise and the unbelievers descent into hell. The Moslem's idea of paradise is one of sensuousness; totally contrary to the biblical account of heaven, wherein is delight in the Lord and worship of Him rather than a continuous gratification of one's own sensuous needs. The Moslem today believes that after the coming of the twelfth Inam, he will be aided by Jesus in forcing the world to accept Islam, then everyone including Jesus will die. Thereafter, a trumpet will sound and all will be raised to life. God will weigh men's actions on a pair of balances to determine which deeds outweigh the other. If a person has fifty-one percent good deeds he will go to heaven; otherwise, he will fall into hell. The Moslem is never sure of salvation at death. His salvation is based on works, and only the day of judgment will tell him his final destiny.

The Christian believes in heaven and hell. Jesus graphically describes hell in his story of the rich man and Lazarus, (Luke 16:19-31). Hell is eternal. Heaven to the Christian is a place of delight, but not in the sense as the Moslem thinks of delight; that being a place of sensuous and sexual pleasure. Heaven, to the Christian is a place of dwelling with God for time and eternity (John 14:1-4).

Since the Moslem does not reckon with sin, he only concerns himself with works. Much has been said in other chapters of this book concerning the Christian belief in sin and in salvation by faith in the atoning work of Christ on the cross. I refer the reader to those chapters.

The Christian knows where he stands eternally with God. The sin question has been settled in his life, and he fears no other judgment; last day or otherwise. A reading of Paul's two epistles to the Thessalonian church will encourage and comfort the Christian concerning the second coming of Jesus Christ.

The Moslem of Iran believes that everyone on earth including Christ will die. He does not believe that Jesus has died already. The Christian knows that Jesus has already died on the cross, and has risen from the dead, and one day He will appear in glory to receive His Church, (1 Thessalonians 4; 13-18). There is no second death for the child of God, and the sting of death has been removed for him (1 Corinthians 15:55-56).

Islam has five pillars besides the doctrines that have been previously described. The pillars are briefly stated. First, there is the recitation of Islam's creed, "There is no God but Allah, and Mohammed is His prophet. Second, prayer must be said five times a day. Third, almsgiving is practiced. Fourth, a month (Ramadan) is given to fasting, and fifth, a pilgrimage to Mecca (the "Hajj") is required of a Moslem at least once in his lifetime.

Circumcision is also practiced. A man may also have four wives if he can afford them. The veiling of women is practiced. No Moslem should gamble or drink alcoholic beverages, nor eat certain meats such as pork.

One can readily see the part that good works play in the Moslem's doctrine of salvation. The beliefs are the constitution, and the pillars are the by-laws of this man-made religion.

Witness to an Islamic

Islam is experiencing great success in the U.S.A., especially among the black race, where it has made great inroads. The only way to resist this religion is to witness. Its adherents are not won through mass evangelistic efforts. They are won to Christ on an individual basis.

In dealing with a Moslem, the Christian must deal with the problem of sin, and talk of a personal relationship with God, rather than a code of rules and regulations. The work is slow, but success can be realized and achieved by prayer and patience.

The reader should seek to obtain a copy of *The Commission, the Foreign Missions Journal of the Southern Baptist Church*, dated September, 1979. It is devoted entirely to the Islamic religion, and gives important data and suggestions on dealing with people of that religion. Copies of this particular journal may be obtained by writing the denomination's headquarters in Nashville, Tennessee.

Notes

[1]Copeland, p. 104.

[2]Millard F. Day, *What's In the Bible?* (Chicago: Moody Press, 1953), pp.91-92.

[3]Clark and Pendleton, p.598.

[4]Boa, p.55.

Bringing The Light Into The Darkness Of World Religions

CHAPTER TEN

Baha'ism

Origin and Founder

Baha'ism is of Persian Mohammedan origin, coming out of the Shiite sect of Islam in 1844 A.D. Mohammed Ali, a heretic of the Islamic faith laid claim to being the "Bab" or "Gate" to divine truth. He was put to death in 1850 because of his insistence to this claim. After his death, one of his followers, Mizra Hussain Ali, upon taking the name of "Baha'ullah," which means "Glory of God," took over the leadership, declaring himself to be the one who was prophesied by the "Bab." His followers changed their name from "Babis" to "Baha'is," thus being named after Baha'ullah.

Baha'ullah used the city of Akka in Palestine as his headquarters. Upon his death, his son, Abbas Effendi, taking the name of Adbul Baha, meaning, "Servant of Baha," assumed leadership.

Beliefs

This world religion seeks to join all religions together. It teaches that the world is one country, and that all people are one. It has world centers in Haifa and Akka, Israel, and in America it has erected a magnificent temple in Wilmette, Illinois, just outside of Chicago. Baha'ism and Theosophy are much similar in their teachings. An implied pantheism comes out of these teachings.[1]

Baha'ism's statement is one of principles rather than one of faith. The author is going to list these principles from two sources. The first list states, "The Oneness of God and Oneness of Religion; The Oneness of mankind; Independent search after Truth; All prejudices must be abandoned (religious, color, national, class, sexual and personal prejudices); International Peace; International Auxiliary Language; Equality for the Sexes; Abolition of Industrial Slavery (Abolition of Wealth and Poverty); Personal Holiness (work in the Spirit of Service is Worship)."[2]

The second source lists the teachings similarly with some important variations. It states, "The oneness of the human race; the independent investigation of truth; the essential oneness of all religions; the ideal of religious unity; the accord of religion with science and reason; the equality of men and women; the abandonment of prejudices; universal peace; universal education;

solution of the economic problem; a universal language; a world tribunal." [3]

These lists of the principles certainly give the reader a vast insight into the mind of the adherent of Baha'ism. The principles, themselves, breathe the doctrine of the "Fatherhood of God and the brotherhood of man". Besides this, they have a tendency to incorporate certain ideas of Karl Marx.

It must be understood that Christianity could never ally itself with Baha'ism because the former rests its case upon faith in Christ, while the latter insists upon reasoning, education and good works. Baha'ism looks upon Christ in the same light as it looks upon any world religious leader. He is accepted with them on an even basis. No distinction is made.

Baha'ism, Theosophy, Modernism and Liberalism are nothing more than tributaries of the great river of thought of Mohammedanism. This is the reason why I have chosen to write about the great religions of the world; first to show their diametrically opposed views to Christianity. and second, to show that the modern cults are nothing more than copies of these great religions.

Witness to a Baha'ist

Baha'ists can be reached with the gospel of Christ. They use an evangelistic approach in converting people to their religion. Christianity must use the same approach on them.

Baha'ism reaches out for the intellectual mind. It presently is pressing hard toward reaching the college youth whose mind thirsts and hungers after spiritual matters. This religion completely removes the idea of sin. Christians, in witnessing to Baha'ists, must show the reality of sin in a person's life regardless of intellectual attainments. Christ must be presented as Superior to all other religious leaders. This can be done by Christians who are willing to hold high the Word of God and present its teaching in a manner that will proclaim Christ as the only Savior of the World. The Holy Spirit will honor and bless such an effort.

CHAPTER ELEVEN

Zoroastrianism

Origin and Founder

The Zoroastrian religion was founded by Zoroaster who was also known by the name of Zarathustra. This Persian prophet's teachings became the guiding light of the great Persian civilization. Two great kings of Persia, whose deeds are prominently recorded in the Old Testament book of Ezra and Nehemiah helped spread the teachings of Zoroaster throughout their vast empire.

The Zoroastrians were forced to leave their homeland because of the intense persecution of their people by the Moslems. They eventually found refuge in India and made this place one of permanent residence. Here they became known as the "Parsees," a word derived from their Persian heritage. Though this religion totals no more than 130,000 members, it has a unique place in religious history.

Not much is known about Zoroaster. He may be dated around 660-583 B.C. Much speculation, myth, and fable surrounds his life. What little information that can be learned about him must be found in the religion's sacred scriptures called the "Avesta," which means knowledge.

At the age of 30, Zoroaster had a vision that convinced him that the truth had been revealed to him so he began his preaching itinerary. At first he was unsuccessful until he converted a Persian king by the name of Kavi Vishtaspa. This was the turning point in Zoroaster's life that he had waited twelve years for, and it was the beginning of the rise of a religion that is closely akin to Judaism and Christianity in some of its beliefs.

One must quickly learn that to understand the Zoroastrian religion one must study the life of Zoroaster. They are inseparable. In a later Zorastrian writing the following information has come to light. It helped deify this personage in the minds of his followers and cause them to worship and adore him.

Notice how his life parallels that of the Life of Jesus Christ who was not to come into the world until a much later date. Zoroaster's birth was prophesied 3000 years prior to its happening.

Added to that prophecy, was the one that he would be a "Savior," and that his birth would be virgin. He is claimed to have been visited by Magi at his birth. At infancy, he was miraculously saved from treachery by jealous people. He disputed theology with noted theologians. He worked miracles, giving sight to the blind and casting out demons. He began his prophetic ministry at age thirty. His message was that of a Supreme God of truth and goodness. He was temped by the devil and finally he was transported to heaven by angels, not having to wait for the Day of Judgment.[1]

The above is fanciful thinking at its very best. It was never Zoroaster's intention to be deified by his followers. As years passed, more myths were added to the already incredible list. The author has brought these myths into his work to show how easy it is for people to be carried away by the devil into avenues of error. There are modern day "prophets" who relish at being considered holy, and because of their lack of scruples, would even be thrilled to be deified by their followers. God's Word warns people of such men. They are called "anti-christs," (1 John 2:18).

Beliefs

The religion of Zoroastrianism greatly changed after the death of its founder. It took on a mystical tone. Dual spirits, good and evil, warred against each other. Finally, Zoroastrians, with a religious theology so complicated and so complex could not decipher the real meaning of their own religion.

Much credit must be given to Zoroaster. He brought to the Gentile world a monotheistic theology. The "Magi" who visited the Christ-child were from the "East," the land of Persia. They were of the Zoroastrian faith.

The following is a glaring fallacy in the teaching of Zoroaster. He believed in hell. However, even he believed that the righteous would go to paradise and the wicked would go to hell. He also believed that the wicked would eventually be purified in hell and at a later date would go to heaven. The Roman Catholic religion similarly believes in this theological concept. It uses the word "purgatory."

The Christian must take exception to this teaching. God's Word clearly stated that hell is a place where the wicked will dwell forever. There is no 'second chance." Scriptures abound in the discussion of hell as a place of permanent residence for the wicked. Jesus clearly explained it in His story of Lazarus and the rich man (Luke 16:19-31). It is the destiny of the wicked.

The doctrine of "Restorationism teaches that punishment in hell is not eternal, but a temporary place for the purpose of purifying the sinner, making him fit for heaven."[2] This sordid doctrine has crept into the Christian theology by falsely interpreting the word "eternal." They contend that the word should be "age long". According to Matthew 25:41, if the punishment of the wicked has an end, so does the bliss of righteousness. There will be no period of restoration or no period of second probation. Man's destiny is fixed at his death (Hebrews 9:27). God will no more force a man to be saved in the future life than he does in the present one.[3]

Witness to a Zoroastrian

The chances of the reader coming into contact with a Zoroastrian may be very slight, but he may very readily come into contact with someone with Zoroastrian beliefs concerning hell and the wicked. My advice is to know the doctrines of salvation, hell, and the destiny of the wicked.

The Christian will also come into contact with people who believe in another Zoroastrian belief that only can bring damnation to the soul. That doctrine is "salvation by good works." It has been discussed in other chapters of this book. It is prevalent in nearly every religion, ancient and modern.

The true Zoroastrian believes that a savior will come into the world. The Christian can show him that the Savior has already come in the person of the Lord Jesus Christ. From this point he can lead the Zoroastrain to a saving knowledge of Jesus, as Paul and Silas did to the Philippian jailer (Acts 16:30-33).

NOTES

[1]Vos, pp.211-212.
[2]Pearlman, pp.386-387.
[3]Pearlman, p.387.

CHAPTER TWELVE

Judaism

Origin

Judaism has no founder. Its authority is not vested in a person, but in God. Its roots are buried in the Old Testament, particularly in the Pentateuch (the five books of laws, which are the first five books of the Old Testament).[1]

It stands firm as a monotheistic religion. "Hear, O Israel: The Lord our God is one Lord" (Deuteronomy 6:4), is the covenant statement of the "children of God." God revealed Himself and His Word to them on Mount Sinai by giving His "Law" to Moses who was to be His instrument in seeing that the Law was to be kept inviolate (Exodus 20:3-17; Deuteronomy 5:7-21).

God's revelation was progressive. It started with Abraham and continued through his son,

Isaac to Isaac's son Jacob (Israel), and his son Joseph, on through the twelve tribes of Israel, and came to a peak on Mount Sinai in so far as the law was concerned; yet, that revelation continued through the sacred works of the prophets showing the coming of the Messiah who would give His life for the sins of the world (Isaiah 53).

When the Messiah finally came, Israel did not accept Him, for they were looking for a kingly Messiah who would conquer all for them through warlike means, rather than through spiritual means. Jesus Christ, the true Messiah, was rejected by His own people. The Jews could not see God's redemptive plan for them in the giving of His only begotten Son who would die vicariously for their sins.

Israel had a rich spiritual heritage. From their nation would come forth the Lord Jesus Christ, the Savior of the world. I wish to delve briefly into the history of the Jews as a people and as a nation, and to view their religious beliefs in the light of the New Testament, and by doing so, endeavor to point out where and how they failed by rejecting the Lord Jesus Christ as their Messiah in His first advent to the earth. By doing this, I may give insight to the Christian witness as to how he may approach the Jew with the gospel message.

It may be stated that God gave Israel the greatest moral and spiritual standard to live by. He never intended for them to attain these standards by their own power. Rather, He promised them that He would always be with them in guiding them by His Spirit.

History of the Children of Israel

After the children of Israel arrived in the "Promised land" under the leadership of Joshua, she began to slowly function as a nation. After Joshua's death, she was ruled by "Judges," some of whose leadership was good and others evil. During this time, the children of Israel experienced God's judgment during periods of her history when she became unruly. The Word of God perfectly describes this period of lawlessness when it declares, "In those days there was no king in Israel but every man did that which was right in his own eyes" (Judges 17: 6, 21:25).

What was right in Israel's eyes was not right in the eyes of God. She always seemed to have the uncanny ability to lapse into spiritual degeneracy by worshiping idols of foreign nations and of committing adultery among her own people and of inter-marrying with those of the foreign powers who were the neighboring enemies. This resulted in the judgment on her in the form of being taken into bondage by these foreign powers.

When she repented, God would give her victory over the foreign powers and she would once again be a sovereign ruler.

From the period of the "Judges," Israel moved into the "Kingdom" era when she sought to be like other nations and demanded to be ruled by a king, even at the displeasure of God (1 Samuel 8:5). It was God's will for Israel that she would be under His rule (theocratic rule) rather than be under a monarchy (rule by kings). God abided by their wishes and their first king was Saul. He was succeeded by David.

Jesus Christ is called the "son of David" by Saint Matthew (Matthew 1:1), and through David's royal line Jesus was born (Matthew 1:16). David was succeeded by his son Solomon, who built the magnificent temple in which the glory of God would rest. Solomon, however, took many of his wives from foreign nations whose religions were polytheistic. Solomon sought after these gods and God judged him and Israel by dividing the nation after his death.

Ten tribes of the nation lived in northern Israel under the kingship of Jeroboam who was the captain of Solomon's army. Their capital was Samaria. Two of the tribes (Judah and Benjamin) remained in the south, ruled by King Rehoboam, who was Solomon's son. Jerusalem remained as their capital.

In the year that followed, the southern kingdom, which was known as Judah, experienced a
number of revivals that resulted in her turning to
God. These occurred because of the preaching of
godly prophets and the leadership of godly kings.

Israel to the north, however, never experienced such spiritual revivals, because neither the
nation nor its kings would listen to the warnings
of God's prophets. Consequently, Israel was taken
captive by the Assyrians around 721 B.C. Hoshea
was on the throne of Israel during this period. In
about 587 B.C., Judah fell to the Babylonian empire. Judah was ruled by Zedekiah.

Even though God had allowed a division to
occur in the great nation of Israel, and from this
division the capture of the two nations by foreign
powers, He still had His hand on her, for out of
Judah would come the Savior of the world, whose
name was Jesus.

One may ask what good resulted from the
division and subsequent capture of Israel and
Judah? To properly answer this question is to
remind the reader that even though Israel was
monotheistic in its belief of God, she and her kings
lapsed into spiritual degeneracy by worshiping
idols. When the Jews returned under Zerubbabel
to Jerusalem by the permission of the Persian
king, Israel never again from that time until now,
indulged herself in idol worship.

During the time under the leadership of Zerubbabel, Ezra and Nehemiah, Judah had a great revival. Her temple was rebuilt, her worship was restored and the city walls of Jerusalem were repaired. Revival resulted because of repentance.

Here the biblical account ends, as far as Israel's history is concerned. Secular history gives details concerning her struggles during the "Maccabean" period. Her biblical history comes to light again at the birth of Jesus Christ, when Israel, having some form of independence, still was under the strong arm of the Roman empire. Christ's mission was to reveal Himself as the true Messiah that Israel was looking for. He claimed the distinction of being the "Son of God". His claim by the political and religious leaders was rejected and the result was His death on Calvary's cross for the sins of all mankind. His resurrection was also disclaimed by the religious leaders.

In 70 A.D., the city of Jerusalem and the temple (known as Herod's temple), was destroyed. Here ended the sacrificial form of worship that Israel knew so well. The Jews were dispersed into many foreign lands; into many persecutions. However, she was once again declared an independent nation on November 29, 1947, when the United Nations voted to end British control of Palestine and to divide the country into a Jewish and an Arab state. Today, her blue and white "Star of David" flag flies high and proud in her nation. God once again has made her a nation united and free. She will undergo more struggles, hardships and persecutions, but she will win, and she will recognize once and for all the true Messiah – the Lord Jesus Christ. This time Israel will not reject Him, but will wholeheartedly accept Him and give Him the rightful place in the lives of its people that He has yearned to have, and deservedly so. In the meantime, it is the duty of every true Christian to love the Jew, to pray for him and to endeavor to witness to him of the saving power of the Lord Jesus Christ.

The Beliefs

The Jews place great emphasis on the study of the Scriptures and religious writings. The Old Testament, which is known as the Hebrew Bible, is the foundation of the Jewish religion. It consists of the Torah, the Prophets, and the writings.

The Torah, or the Law, as it is known to the Jews, serves as the religious foundation for the Jewish faith. This book consists of the Pentateuch, which contains the five books of Moses, namely, Genesis, Exodus, Leviticus, Numbers, and Deuteronomy. These books record the history of the Jewish people from creation through the death of Moses. It must be impressed on the reader that the Torah is most vital to the Jewish religion as it contains the basic laws and the Ten Commandments to which the true religious believer follows with great care.

The Prophets give the account of the Jews as a people and a nation. These prophets heralded the words of God which could be words of comfort or words of impending judgment.

The Writings contain the poetic works, the proverbs, the psalms and the historical works. The Talmud is made up of the Mishnah and the Gemara. The Mishnah contains the oral laws of the rabbis which are just as binding as the written Law, and the Gemara is the recording of the discussion and the interpretation of the Mishnah. This work serves as the guide to the civil and religious laws and teachings of Judaism.

During Jesus' life on earth, Judaism had grown into a religion of two major sects or factions. The Pharisees, which came out of the Maccabean period, were a sect which believed in the supernatural. They believed in angels and the resurrection of the dead. The Sadducees on the other hand, rejected the belief of the Pharisees. Jesus was constantly at odds with these two factions. The Pharisees, especially, had compounded laws upon laws on the people which put them under a spiritual and religious yoke of bond-age. Jesus repudiated these teachings as binding on the people. It was the Pharisees and the Sadducees who constantly under-minded the work of Christ, and who were instrumental in His death. Evil in that day, though they may have been, God used them in His redemptive plan for Israel and the entire human race. He provided a Sacrifice for sin, and all that it takes, is to believe in that Sacrifice, who is Jesus, and be saved. It must, however, be done on a personal basis.

The true Jewish believer holds the Sabbath in high esteem. It begins at sunset on Friday and ends at sunset on Saturday. Circumcision of the male child on the eighth day, is a ceremony that is still adhered to by all Jews today.

The Jewish religion took the great leap from a religion of sacrifices to one of teachings and tra-ditions after the Temple was destroyed by the Romans in 70 A.D. Today, there are three major groups of Judaism. First, there is the Orthodox group which adheres to the Torah's every word. It observes all the ceremonial rites and holy days. Second, there is the Conservative group which stresses the unity of all Jewish groups. The third group, is the Reform group which is the liberal part of Judaism.

The synagogue is the meeting place for all Jewish people. Here is where they worship God.

It came into prominence during Ezra's time and since the destruction of the Temple in 70 A.D., it is not only the place of worship, but also the teaching center of the Jewish faith. Synagogues can be found in practically every city where Jews live. The rabbi or teacher is the spiritual head of the synagogue, and he leads the people in their worship services.

The Jewish male is highly considered. When a boy reaches the age of thirteen years, he becomes "Bar Mitzvah," or "son of the commandment." There is also a ceremony for the girl in which she becomes "Bat Mitzvah," or daughter of the commandment."

The Jews do not like one of their own marrying anyone outside the Jewish faith. They are a very closely knit people, not only because it is by commandment of God, but also because of their tremendous persecutions.

There are many Jewish fasts and feasts. Two of the most notable are "Yon Kippur," This is the Day of Atonement, the holiest day of the Jewish year. The other is the "Passover," which is a festival of Freedom, bringing to mind the exodus of the children of Israel from Egypt.

A Jew, though he may not be religious, will fight to retain his true identity as a Jew. He feels that there is no need for conversion because he was born into the "Family of God," and by nature of this birth, he will always be a Jew—a child of God.

For a Jew to become a Christian convert means the losing of family and friends. They totally reject him and forsake him as if he were never born. It takes much love and prayer to win a Jew to Christ, for his opinion of Christianity is justly one of hate and despising, as history well bears out.

Witness to a Jew

Judaism denies the sin nature of man, and therefore, minimizes man's need of redemption. When a Jew falls away from his faith, all that he must do is repent or come back to God through his faith. Christ is given no place in the Jewish economy. "The Jew has a zeal of God, but not according to knowledge" (Romans 10:2).

The Jew's religion is called the "Jewish " religion. His language is "Hebrew," and his nationality is "Israelite." In terms of prophecy, he is God's timepiece.

Though the New Testament is not in the canon of the Hebrew Scriptures, it does not mean to say that Christ is not in the Hebrew Scriptures. The Christian may open the Old Testament and reveal Christ to the Jew. Here he will learn that this Messiah will be born in Bethlehem (Micah 5:

2), and that a virgin will give birth to Him, (Isaiah 7:14). In Psalm 2:7 and 2:12; Jesus is shown as the Son of God. Isaiah 9:26, declares that He is God and man. Isaiah 53:5,6 and Daniel 9:26, shows that Jesus is the sacrifice for the sins of others, and the Jews will know him by His wounds, as recorded in Zechariah 12:10 and 13:6.

The Old Testament predicts two Messianic advents, The Orthodox, repeats religiously every morning these words in his prayer, "I believe with a firm faith in the coming of the Messiah and although He tarry, yet will I wait for Him till He comes." He believes that at the coming of the Messiah the national hopes of Israel will be fulfilled. He finds this to be so in the following scriptures, Psalm 102:16; Isaiah 9:7; Micah 4:3. The Jew will note that since such prophecies have not as yet been fulfilled, the Messiah has not as yet come. It is evident the Messiah will come to literally fulfill such prophecies as have been mentioned, referring to His reign on earth. He has already come to fulfill numerous other prophecies referring to His sacrificial death as an atonement for sin. Isaiah 11 refers to the second coming of the Messiah, but the Jew must not overlook Isaiah 53, which has been literally fulfilled in Jesus Christ.

The Jew should be asked to give careful study to Isaiah 53. This chapter is not read in the synagogue. If a rabbi is consulted concerning this chapter, he states that if refers to the sufferings of Israel. He substitutes the word "Israel" wherever the pronoun "He" is used. If "He" refers to Israel, then to whom does "we" refer? Compare Psalm 22. In Isaiah 53:5,6, the sense of the verses will be made clear if the word "Messiah" or "Jesus" is used in place of "Israel."

The Jew should be made aware that his nation rejected Christ at His first coming. Again Isaiah 53 is referred to, together with Psalm 18: 22. These depict the attitude that the Jews had toward Jesus. The biblical story of Joseph and his brothers, and of their attitude, may be given to illustrate Israel's attitude toward Jesus at His first coming.

The Jew needs to know above all things that he, too, is a sinner, and that he needs atonement for his sin as does every other living person on earth. His protest to such a declaration does not change the fact. He must be reminded of the celebration of the Day of Atonement. At this time, the Orthodox Jew swings a fowl over his head and repeats, "This is my substitute. This fowl goes to eternal death and I to eternal life." By showing this to the Jew, he is reminded that he really does need a sacrifice for sin.

The Christian witness may use Jeremiah 31: 31, 33 in answer to the question of the Jew about keeping the laws and ceremonies of his religion. The Jew must be asked to read the New Testament. In light of the explanation of Isaiah 53, and his curiosity of its explanation in terms of the Messiah, and of Jesus being that Messiah, he might be more willing to read the New Testament to quench the thirst and hunger of that curiosity.

It must be explained to the Jew that the key to the Old Testament is the New Testament, and that it will prove that Jesus is the One "of whom Moses in the law and the prophets did write," (John 1:45).

Commit the results to God. The Jew needs a double conversion; a "head conversion" and a " heart conversion." It may take months or even years before a Jew truly receives Jesus Christ as his Lord and Savior, though his conversion may be almost instantaneous, "For there is life for a look at the Crucified one."

The seed will be sown. The reaping, by the power and illumination of the Holy Spirit will come to pass (Romans 1:16). It is the responsibility and the privilege of every Christian believer to be a light and a witness to the Jew of the saving power of the Lord Jesus Christ.

I feel it necessary to give a word of caution in giving the Jew tracts concerning Jesus Christ. Do not use any literature that has the sign or symbol of the cross imprinted on it. It reminds the Jew of persecution. In the same manner, it is not wise to speak of the "Christ of the cross." Explain what the word "Christian" means. Simply, use terms and phrases that are known and understandable to the Jew that are found in the Old Testament.

The chapter, entitled *The Roman Road*, will prove invaluable in witnessing to the Jew or anyone who is a member of any of the great religions which have been discussed in this book, or to anyone whose religion or cult have not been discussed in this book.

Notes
[1]Vos, p.39

CHAPTER THIRTEEN

Christianity

It would be most improper not to include Christianity among the world religions in this book, for it is the most widespread religion in the world, with over one billion followers. It has been the major force in the moral and religious fiber of many of the nations of the world.

Origin and Founder

Jesus Christ founded Christianity. His ministry began in Palestine, where He taught and preached the "Kingdom of God". He chose twelve disciples (followers) whom He called "apostles" or "ones sent". They assisted Him in His work. Actually, the Lord was preparing them to carry on His teachings after His ascension into heaven.

The message of Christ was a simple one. He taught and preached that He was the Son of God and the Savior of men, and through Him only, could a man be saved.

Jesus Christ was born sinless (of a virgin), and conceived by the Holy Ghost. He healed the sick and cast out demons. Everywhere He went, Christ glorified His heavenly Father.

His infinite love for mankind was shown in His vicarious death on the cross. He arose from the dead on the third day as He had said. He appeared to many and finally He ascended into heaven to be with His heavenly Father from whence He came.

Just prior to His ascension into heaven, Jesus commanded His disciples to go to Jerusalem to be filled with the Holy Ghost. They obeyed Him, and on the Day of Pentecost, one hundred twenty of the followers of Christ were filled with the Holy Ghost and went forth from there as His first messengers.

The Holy Bible is the sacred book of the Christian religion. It contains sixty-six books. Thirty-nine of the books (Genesis to Malachi) are contained in what is known as the "Old Testament." These books are also in the Jewish religion's canon of sacred scriptures. The New Testament has twenty-seven books (Matthew to Revelation). The Jewish religion does not accept the New Testament, as they do not accept Christ as the Messiah or the "Anointed One." The sixty-six books of the Holy Bible are in the Christian religion's canon of sacred Scripture. Many Christians hold these sacred works to be inspired of God; that is given to men directly from God.

There is another set of books, called the "Apocrypha' or the "hidden books." These books are not considered as in the canon of Scripture with the above mentioned books. They do, however, carry some historical information of the Jews during what is known as the "inter-testamental" period; that is the period between the writing of Malachi's prophecy and the gospel texts of the New Testament. This period covers approximately 450 years. Other of these books are of no important spiritual value as they do not concur with the accepted works that are considered in the canon. The Roman Catholic Church maintains that there is a spiritual value to these books and still include them in their canon of Scripture.

A detailed study on the Christian religion is too far reaching in its history and doctrine, therefore, I will only give a synopsis of the religion. Christianity began with Jesus Christ. Christianity is Jesus Christ. It is absolutely nothing without Him. Paul, the great apostle, in each of his epistles (letters) teaches and preaches Jesus Christ. His main thrust is a gospel of redemption. His doctrinal position is Jesus Christ, the Savior of the world.

Beliefs

The major doctrines or teachings of Christianity center around Christ. These doctrines include His virgin birth, sinless life, miraculous power, His vicarious death on the cross, noting that He purposely gave His life for the sins of mankind, His resurrection from the dead, His ascension into Heaven and His soon coming for the true Church.

Christianity has gone through the fire of persecution, yet it has come forth triumphant because its messengers would not yield to the dictating powers of the ungodly world. It maintained its stand on righteousness, holiness and godliness. It would not relinquish the doctrine of the deity of Jesus Christ, neither would it avow that there is no hell or deny that there is a heaven.

The Roman Empire tried to extinguish the light of Christianity, but men of the character and persuasion of Paul would not let that light be extinguished. Christianity had a period of reprieve from persecution during the rule of Emperor Constantine of Rome.

Christianity remained a unified and powerful religion for the most part for about one thousand years. In the 800's, a division (schism) occurred and it began to split the church at Rome and at Constantinople. This split resulted in a final separation of the Roman Catholic Church which was headquartered at Rome, and the Eastern Orthodox Church which held Constantinople as its headquarters.

In the 1500's, many large groups of Christians began to dissent from the Roman Catholic Church . These groups became known as "Protestants," and the period of dissension was known as the "Reformation." Martin Luther was a major force in this reformation period. The Protestants protested over religious matters. They felt that the Church had become too worldly in its power.

Three major divisions of Christianity

Today, Christianity includes three major divisions. First, there is the Roman Catholic Church; second, there is also the Eastern Orthodox Church, and third, there is the Protestant Church. The Protestant Church, however has many denominations and sects.

The estimated membership of each of the three divisions of Christianity are as follows: The Roman Catholic Church has approximately 1,077,000,000 members. They are followed by the Protestant group which approximates 400,000,000 members. Lastly, the Eastern Orthodox has about 218,000,000 members.[1]

Roman Catholic Church Beliefs

The Roman Catholic Church receives the Holy Bible as the inspired Word of God (though it includes the Apocrypha), together with the traditions and teachings of the church, which were handed down by the various popes who are the spiritual leaders of the church.

The Roman Catholic Church believes in the virgin birth of Christ. However, they carry this doctrine to the extreme in placing Mary in a mediatorial position; that is, they pray to God through her, in hopes of receiving divine favors from Christ. They uphold the celibacy (priests not allowed to be married) of the priesthood. This Church believes that the Virgin Mary ascended into heaven as Jesus did, without dying. It also holds the priest in high esteem. He is the "Father Confessor" of the people. He can give absolution for sins.

The people of the Roman Catholic faith pray to the saints since deceased, for favors. Each saint has a certain authority or power while in heaven in order to grant specific favors. Besides Mary, who is a saint, Paul holds that position together with Peter, who is the "Rock" of the Church, and all the apostles and many others who have had alleged miracles attending their ministry.

The Roman Catholic Church believes that the literal body and blood of Christ are in the wine and wafer that is given to the faithful at the Holy Communion service. This doctrine is called "transubstantiation". It happens when the priest blesses the "Eucharist" (the sacrament of bread and wine).

The Roman Catholic Church believes in "purgatory," which is a temporary residence for the faithful of the church to be purged from all sin so that they may enter heaven. The living church members have prayers said for those in purgatory. The confession of sins during one's lifetime seems never to be sufficient to enter heaven immediately upon death.

The pope (which means "father") is the spiritual head of the church. He is claimed to be the vicar of Christ on earth. He is declared to be in direct line from Saint Peter, who was the Church's first pope. The pope is infallible in matters spiritual and moral in the Roman Catholic Church.

The author has listed only a few of the major doctrines of the Catholic Church. It is not difficult for the evangelical Christian to disagree with those doctrines for they are not taught in the Word of God.

Roman Catholics can and are won to Jesus Christ. When I lived in the city of Montreal in Canada where the major portion of the population was of that religious persuasion, I saw many find Jesus Christ as personal Savior in their lives.

Witness to a Roman Catholic

To win a Roman Catholic to Christ is not to argue with him, but in love, show him the true meaning of the death of Jesus Christ. The Catholic knows how to pray, even beyond the recitation of certain required prayers of the church. He can pray a prayer of confession of sins to Christ if he is properly led. One must remember that the Catholic was born a Catholic. He was taught in parochial schools by nuns and priests. He believes in the Catholic faith as it is presented to him in his catechism. To change his faith may take many months and years of soul searching, but a change can be effected by the power of the Holy Spirit and a consecrated Christian witness.

Eastern Orthodox Church Beliefs

The Eastern Orthodox Churches are the major Christian churches in Greece, Russia, and Eastern Europe together with Western Asia. This great church in Christendom has a clergy made up of three major orders; the bishops, priests and deacons. The priests are allowed to marry, although there are those who belong to the monastic clergy. It must be noted that married priests took on their marital vows before ordination. They were not permitted to marry after they took their ordination vows. Only unmarried priests can become bishops.

The Holy Bible and other holy traditions make up the major teachings of the church. They do not believe in the infallibility of a person. This communion believes that the Holy Spirit proceeds from the Father (John 15: 26), while the Western Roman Catholic Church and the Protestant mainline churches take the position that the Holy Spirit proceeds from the Father and from the Son.

The Eastern Orthodox Church believes in the sacrament of confession or penance, where the penitent confesses his sins to God in the presence of a priest who forgives the sins in the name of God and offers spiritual counsel to the penitent. The Eastern Orthodox Church, unlike the Roman Catholic Church in many of the ecclesiastical dogmas, still shares with it a similarity in liturgical forms of worship.

One is born into the Eastern Orthodox Church as one is born into the Roman Catholic Church. Infant baptism is practiced and there is a period in the child's life (around six years of age) when he is taken into the membership of the church by means of confirmation when it is blessed by the bishop who is the presiding official over such a spiritual ceremony. Infant baptism relates itself with baptismal regeneration which means that at the time a child is baptized, it is saved.

The early Christian church never taught such a doctrine as baptismal regeneration, and neither does the Word of God. Nicodemus was a ruler of the Jews. He was born into Judaism, yet Christ told him of the need of the "new birth" (John 3:3). Paul, that great apostle of the Christian faith, had to have a spiritual re-birth to become a Christian (Acts 9:1-8). Therefore, to be a Christian, one must also have a spiritual re-birth; a spiritual conversion; a confession of sin and act of repentance and acceptance of Jesus Christ as Lord and Savior. One must personally commit one's life to Christ to be saved. No church or dogma or tradition or ceremonial rite can redeem a lost soul. Only Jesus Christ has the authority to forgive sins. This authority is not vested in any person, pope, bishop, priest, minister or patriarch.

Witness to an Eastern Orthodox

One wins a member of the Eastern Orthodox Church in the same manner and by using the same methods as one would use in witnessing to a Roman Catholic.

The Protestant Church

The third great division in Christianity is the Protestant Church. It cannot really be called a church as such, for so many churches of so many different theological beliefs meld together in what is called Protestantism.

There is the Episcopal Church, the Methodist Church, the Presbyterian Church, the Lutheran Church, the Baptist Church. Even within these major denominations, there are divisions. Besides the Episcopal Church, there is the Reformed Episcopal church. The Baptists have the Southern Baptist Convention, the Regular Baptists and the Seventh-Day Baptists, just to name a few. The Lutherans, Methodists and Presbyterians follow along the same lines.

From one or more of these denominations, others were born. There is the Church of the Nazarene, The Disciples of Christ and The Christian and Missionary Alliance. The Pentecostals are represented by the Assemblies of God, Pentecostal Holiness Church, Church of God, Church of God in Christ, Four Square Gospel and a host of others with various names.

Belief

Each of the above named churches claim a special distinction for its existence. Each has its own ecclesiastical authority and polity. Each has its own distinctive method of worship and beliefs.

I appreciate these different church denominations within the Protestant and Christian community; however, I also insist that these churches have no authority to claim salvation for any of their members on the basis of church member-ship. The Biblical teaching of the "New Birth" must be maintained in these churches' disciplines and it must be preached from their pulpits or else their members are as lost as any believer in Is-lam, Hinduism, Buddhism or any non-Christian religion.

As a final note, many of the cults today are trying to infiltrate the major denominations and win from them converts doomed for hell. These cults are too many in name and number to men-tion in this work. However, if the Christian reader will give careful study to the major non-Christian religions, he will see the underlying beliefs in the cults, and he will be able to deal with these cult members as he would one on one of the non-Chris-tian religions.

Witness to the Protestant Faith

Witnessing to a member of any church in any of the many churches within the great Protestant community must be done on the basis of a member's acceptance of Jesus Christ as Lord and Savior of ones life, and not on church member-ship. Use the "Roman Road" as a guide in wit-nessing to an unsaved person who is a member of one of these churches.

Notes

[1] *The Information Please Almanac*, 2004 edition, p.612.

CHAPTER FOURTEEN

Conclusion

In conclusion, I have presented a work on the major world religions with a hope that it will stimulate interest in the minds of Christian witnesses and challenge their hearts to further study in this most important subject to the point that they will become expert not only in the subject matter of world religions, but also in the methods of winning adherents of these world religions to a saving knowledge of the Lord Jesus Christ. Knowledge is power. It gives authority. To have a knowledge of the beliefs of the major world religions gives the Christian witness a certain power in terms of a respectable understanding of the beliefs of these major world religions. And with this power, an authority to speak intelligently to their adherents.

Notwithstanding, the Christian also needs to have a proper understanding of the Word of God and the doctrines of the Christian faith that it teaches. This will enable him to work with a greater degree of success in his task of witnessing.

It must never be forgotten, however, that the Christian witness must always be led by the Holy Spirit, therefore, he must continually study the Word of God and be in much prayer so that his life will be an example of the Christ life.

The reader should study each chapter of this work carefully. Take into mind the origin and founder of the religion and the reason for believing the way he does. Note how he propagates his message. Study his beliefs and the sources of his beliefs. This will assist the Christian immeasurably in dealing with an adherent of a major world religion.

The reader may further be helped by comparing a major world religion with Christianity in the truest theological sense. To do this, the reader needs to study the religion's belief in salvation and how it is to be obtained, then compare this doctrine with that of Christianity. Follow this method in studying the religion's beliefs in the doctrines of God, holy living and life in the hereafter.

If the religion has come into existence after Christianity, study its understanding of the person of Jesus Christ and His teachings. If the religion originated before the time of Christ, study its beliefs concerning the person of Jesus Christ as presented by its present day adherents.

The Christian witness will readily see after reading this book, that I have endeavored to cover much of the subject matter that I propose the reader to study in order to have an intelligent understanding of the beliefs of the major world religions. Give careful consideration of Appendix A of this work. It will help the Christian witness to be systematic in his approach to witnessing to another person, regardless of his religious beliefs. *The Roman Road* methods have been used with much success by the serious minded Christian witness.

Finally, I suggest that other important works on this massive subject be sought out and studied. Then from the knowledge gained from this study, the reader may in turn pass on his knowledge by submitting it in his academic writings. This added information will give a storehouse of knowledge in a field that is of vital importance to every dedicated Christian witness.

Important as it is to know the beliefs of major world religions, equally important is it to know the methods of presenting the Christian Gospel to their adherents.

I sincerely hope that this work will be a stimulus to other men of God to add their writings on this subject and thus help in the world evangelism of the lost.

THE ROMAN ROAD

Author's Notes

I wish to include a simple plan for witnessing to the lost. It is not a new or personally devised plan, but it is one that I have used with good success. It explains the plan of salvation in the most simple manner.

One will readily notice that the plan shows that no one is righteous. It also talks about sin and its consequences. The plan also shows who Jesus is and how He forgives sin.

The reader needs a Bible, or just the New Testament portion of the Bible. I believe that the Christian witness should always carry the whole Bible. The Christian witness may make a road map in his Bible. After marking the first text which is Romans 3:10, state beside that text, "go to number two, which is Romans 3:23" and so on.

When the Christian witness has led a person to Christ, he should follow up his new convert to Christ by making sure that the person goes to church with him personally. He should introduce that person to the pastor of the church and continue going to church with him, especially making sure that he attends Bible study and prayer services, until the new convert has received sufficient grounding to continue serving his Lord on his own.

APPENDIX "A'
(THE ROMAN ROAD TO SALVATION)

START:

    1. (Romans 3:10) There is none righteous.
    [10]As it is written, there is none righteous, no, not one:

GO TO:

    2. (Romans 3:23) All have sinned.
    [23]For all have sinned, and come short of the glory of God.

GO TO:

    3. (Romans 6:23a) The price or wages of sin.
    [23a]For the wages of sin is death:

GO TO:

    4. (Romans 5:8) Jesus paid the price by dying for our sins.
    [8]But God commendeth His love toward us, in that, while we were yet sinners, Christ died for us.

AND:

    5. (John 3:16) Jesus paid the price by dying for our sins.
    [16]For God so loved the world, that He gave His only begotten Son, that whosoever believeth in Him should not perish, but have everlasting life.

GO TO:

6. (Romans 6:23b)   The gift of God is eternal life.

    23b But the gift of God is eternal life through Jesus Christ our Lord.

AND:

7. (Ephesians 2:8-9) The Gift of God is eternal life.

    8 For by grace are ye saved through faith; and that not of yourselves; it is the gift of God;

    9 Not of works, lest any man should boast.

GO TO:

8. (Romans 10:9-13)   Confess Jesus as Savior.

    9 That if thou shalt confess with thy mouth the Lord Jesus, and shalt believe in thine heart that God hath raised Him from the dead, thou shalt be saved.

    10 For with the heart man believeth unto righteousness; and with the mouth confession is made unto salvation.

    11 For the Scripture saith, whosoever believeth on Him shall not be ashamed.

    12 For there is no difference between the Jew and the Greek; for the same Lord over all is rich unto all that call upon Him.

[13]*For whosoever shall call upon the Name of the Lord shall be saved.*

GO TO:

9. (Matthew 28:19-20) Be baptized in water.

   [19]*Go ye therefore, and teach all nations, baptising them in the name of the Father, and of the Son, and of the Holy Ghost.* [20]*Teaching them to observe all things whatsoever I have commanded you: and, Lo, I am with you always, even to the end of the world. Amen.*

Estimated Membership of the Principal Religions of the World

Religion	World Total
Total Christian	2,038,905,000
Jewish	14,535,000
Moslem	1,226,403,300
Zoroastrian	1,096,000
Shinto	2,703,000
Taoist	2,659,000
Confucian	6,327,000
Buddhist	364,014,000
Hinduism	4,345,000
Grand Total	3,660,987,000

Statistics of the great religions of the world are only rough estimates. Each religion has its own method of taking its census, and these cannot in any way be counted accurate.

The total Christian membership includes Roman Catholic, Eastern Orthodox and Protestant.

The Jewish religious figures relate to the total Jewish population whether or not related to the synagogue.

Because of war and persecution, there are about 18,600,000 refugees throughout the world who are not integrated into religious statistics of the land of their temporary residence.

The source from which the population figures of the great religions of the world was derived from, is the 2004 edition of *Information Please Almanac*, which is published by the Information Please Publishing, Incorporation, New York, New York.

Bibliography

Bancroft, Emery H. *Christian Theology.* Grand Rapids: Zondervan Publishing House, 1949.

Berkhof, L. *Systematic Theology.* Grand Rapids: Wm. B. Eerdmans Publishing Company, 1977.

Boa, Kenneth. *Cults, World Religions, and You.* Wheaton: Victor Books, 1978.

Carnell, Edward John. *An Introduction to Christian Apologetics.* Grand Rapids: Wm.B. Eerdmans Publishing Company, 1966.

Clarke, Adam. *A Commentary on the Whole Bible.* 6 vols. Cincinnati: Applegate and Company,1854.

Conner, Walter T. *The Gospel of Redemption.* Nashville: Broadman Press,1963.

Copeland, E. Luther. *Christianity and World Religions.* Nashville: Broadman Press, 1963.

Crawford, Percy B. *The Art of Fishing for Men.* Chicago: Moody Press,1950.

Criswell, W. A. *Why I Preach that the Bible is Literally True.* Nashville: Broadman Press, 1969.

Day, Millard F. *What's In the Bible.* Chicago: Moody Press, 1953.

Evans William. *Personal Soul-Winning.* Chicago: Moody Press, 1948.

Fisher, George Park. *Manual of Christian Evidences*. Pennsylvania: Charles Scribner's Sons, 1888.

Foxe, John. *Christian Martyrs of the World*. Chicago: Moody Press, 1949.

Halley, Henry H. *Pocket Bible Handbook*. Chicago: Henry H. Halley Publisher, 1951.

Harrison, Everett F. *A Short Life of Christ*. Grand Rapids: Wm. B. Eerdmans Publishing Company, 1968.

Hough, Robert Ervin. *The Christian After Death*. Chicago: Moody Press, 1947.

Information Please Almanac, New York: Information Please Publishing Inc.

Jamieson, Robert, A. R. Fausset and David Brown. *Commentary on the Whole Bible*. 1 vol. Grand Rapids: Zondervan Publishing House, 1949.

Larkin, Clarence. *The Spirit World*. Philadelphia: Rev. Clarence Estates, 1921.

Latourette, Kenneth Scott. *A History of Christianity*. New York: Harper and Brothers Publishers, 1953.

McDill, Wayne. *Evangelism In a Tangled World*. Nashville: Broadman Press, 1976.

Means, Pat. *The Mystical Maze*. San Bernardion: Campus Crusade for Christ, Inc., 1976.

Munro, W, Fraser. *A Brief Dictionary of the Denominations.* Nashville:Broadman Press, 1964.

Nave, Orville, J. *Nave's Topical Bible.* Chicago: Moody Press, 1921.

Osborrne, T. L. *Soulwinning.* Tulsa: T. L. Osborne Evangelistic Association Publishers, 1967.

Pearlman, Myer. *Knowing the Doctrines of the Bible.* Missouri: The Gospel Publishing House, 1937.

Pendleton, J. M. and George W. Clark. *The New Testament With Brief Notes.* Chicago:The Judson Press, 1949.

Pink, Arthur W. *The Attributes of God.* Grand Rapids: Baker Book House, 1977.

Schweitzer, Frederick M. *A History of the Jews.* New York: The MacMillian Company, 1971.

Scofield, C. I. *The New Scofield Reference Bible.* New York: Oxford University Press, 1967.

Smith, William. *Smith's Bible Dictionary.* New York: Pyramid Books, 1967.

Strong, James. *The Exhaustive Concordance of the Bible.* New York: Abingdon-Cokesbury Press, 1933.

Thomas, W. H. Griffith. *How We Got Our Bible.* Chicago: Moody Press, 1926.

Turner, J. Clyde. *Soul-Winning Doctrines.* Nashville: Convention Press, 1955.

Unger, Merrill F. *Biblical Demonology.* Wheaton: Van Kampen Press, 1953.

Van Baalen, Jan Karel. *The Chaos of Cults.* Grand Rapids: Wm. Eerdmans Publishing Company, 1953.

Vincent, M. R. *Word Studies in the New Testament.* Delaware: Associated Publishers and Authors, 1972.

Vos, Howard F. *Religions in a Changing World.* Chicago: Moody Press, 1966.

Zwemer, Samuel M. *The Origin of Religion.* New York: Loizeaux Brothers, 1945.